The Bullsh*t-Free Guide to Depression

of related interest

The CBT Art Workbook for Coping with Depression
Jennifer Guest
ISBN 978 1 78775 096 8
eISBN 978 1 78775097 5
CBT Art Workbooks for Mental and Emotional Wellbeing

The Depression Journal
Creative Activities to Keep Yourself Well
Cara Lisette and Sophia Kaur Badhan
Illustrated by Victoria Barron
Foreword by Jonathan Stea
ISBN 978 1 80501 411 9
eISBN 978 1 80501 412 6
Creative Journals for Mental Health

The Recovery Letters
Addressed to People Experiencing Depression
Edited by James Withey and Olivia Sagan
Afterword by Tom Couser
ISBN 978 1 78592 183 4
eISBN 978 1 78450 460 1

What I Do to Get Through
How to Run, Swim, Cycle, Sew or Sing Your Way Through Depression
Edited by Olivia Sagan and James Withey
Foreword by Cathy Rentzenbrink
ISBN 978 1 78775 298 6
eISBN 978 1 78775 299 3

The Bullsh*t-Free Guide to Depression

How to Get Out of Your Mental Health Hole (from someone who has fallen down one or two)

Jacs Guderley

Foreword by Dr Emma Hepburn

Illustrated by Jacs Guderley

Jessica Kingsley Publishers

London and Philadelphia

First published in Great Britain in 2026 by Jessica Kingsley Publishers
An imprint of John Murray Press

2

A CIP catalogue record for this title is available from the British Library and the Library of Congress

ISBN 978 1 83997 701 5
eISBN 978 1 83997 702 2

Printed and bound in the United States by Integrated Books International

Jessica Kingsley Publishers' policy is to use papers that are natural, renewable and recyclable products and made from wood grown in sustainable forests. The logging and manufacturing processes are expected to conform to the environmental regulations of the country of origin.

Jessica Kingsley Publishers
Carmelite House
50 Victoria Embankment
London EC4Y 0DZ
www.jkp.com

John Murray Press
Part of Hodder & Stoughton Ltd
An Hachette Company

The authorised representative in the EEA is Hachette Ireland,
8 Castlecourt Centre, Dublin 15, D15 XTP3, Ireland (email: info@hbgi.ie)

In memory of my darling friend, Ashley – keep on dancing.

Contents

Author's note

My illustrations are all drawn by hand, with pen and paper. They're not made to be perfect, and none of them are – just like our mental health, there is a unique beauty in their imperfections.

Foreword

The human brain is a meaning-making machine. Throughout human history we have created meaning for ourselves through stories. Stories help us make sense of ourselves, the world and our place in the world. Stories connect us and normalize our experiences. Through my work, as clinical psychologist over 20 years, I have seen the power of stories around mental health and the positive impact these can have. Stories of our difficult moments are the hardest to tell, but I would argue the most important and powerful. These stories make sense of our darkest and most puzzling times and in doing so they guide us through, and can even show us, the paths forward.

However, stories of tough times are hard to share. When we fall into a depression hole, we want to shrink and hide, not reveal our stories. Especially when you are Chief President of the club for people who found it difficult to tell others about their depression (as Jacs was). Despite the fact her brain told her not to, Jacs has chosen to share her story of some of her most difficult times. With insight, empathy and humour, she takes us through her dances with depression and invites us into her story to join her 'I've been depressed/I am depressed/I might be depressed/My friend or family member is depressed' club. And we know from the data that this is a big club – the majority of humans will join it at some point in their life. In opening her world, and letting us climb in (then out of) her depression hole, she uses the power of her story to connect with, destigmatize, empathize and understand depression and learn how to respond to it (in both ourselves and others).

By joining Jacs' club, and connecting to the red thread of people who have experienced depression, you will be treated to a fun and lively dance through her tango, waltz, cha cha cha, bachata, west coast swing, jive and Lindy Hop dances with depression (her seven sassy times of being depressed, as she says). Although depression is never fun, Jacs takes you by the hand onto the depression dance floor and through her light-hearted humour and illuminating illustrations, helps you find glimmers of brightness to guide you out of the hole. By putting her own depression in the spotlight, she brings this often unspoken topic to life. Throughout the book she shares her experiences and what she has learnt through her many dances with depression and the therapy she has undertaken. The book is brought to life with her clever illustrations and her ingenious depression inventions, which capture the complexity of depression in ways that will stay with you, imprinted in your brain, to help you long after you have finished reading the book.

But Jacs is not just a storyteller. She is a shame buster and demystifier. By exposing her shame, she helps you (as her Brené Brown quote says) douse your own shame with empathy, so that shame loses its power and begins to wither. She shows that depression is a shared (and common) human experience and that you are not alone – you are connected via your story (and the red threads) to a vast amount of people.

In the process of shame busting, she also opens the doors to her therapy room to demystify the process. Her experience of therapy is central to her story and provides insights into what actually happens during therapy. People are often scared of asking for help and I believe the way Jacs openly shares her therapy experience will help people understand this better and overcome barriers to seeking support.

Having worked with several hundred people with depression over the course of my career, I have always sought stories to help them make sense of their experiences. I am really pleased to now have Jacs' story in my toolkit. I will be recommending Jacs' book to individuals and families to help connect them and guide them through their depression hole to find their light again.

Now (even if depression doesn't make you feel like it), get your dancing shoes on and get ready to hit the depression dance floor with Jacs' story. Don't worry if you think you can't dance, she'll take you by the hand and guide you through the steps with empathy and kindness. You will feel the power of her story, laugh along at her anecdotes and be drawn into her illustrations. Her words and images are points of light that can help guide you through a depression hole, busting shame along the way. By the time the music has finished you'll understand depression better and how to get help, and what you can do when it hits, whether that's in yourself or someone you love.

I'm going to leave the final words here to Jacs: 'Let depression do its worst. We can get through it together, guided by a communal love, empathy and understanding – for ourselves and each other.' Her book will help you do just that.

Dr Emma Hepburn
Clinical psychologist, author and illustrator of *A Toolkit for Modern Life*, *A Toolkit for Happiness* and *A Toolkit for Your Emotions*
@thepsychologymum

* **CHAPTER 1** *

Getting to Know Depression

My story

My mental health story starts with frantically waking my mum and dad in the middle of the night, to tell them I was dying.

You might know that a panic attack can feel like having a heart attack. I didn't know this, and my parents didn't know this. So, panic-stricken at the sight of their hysterical daughter, my parents phoned an ambulance. I was whisked off to A&E, where they told me, 'You're just very depressed.' Okay, thanks – I guess I'll take these anti-depressants and be on my way. I left confused, scared and convinced the doctor's words weren't true.

MY MENTAL HEALTH JOURNEY

I didn't know this was the start of my mental health journey. Once an experience full of shame and fear, and one that I thought I'd never learn to control, I did all I could to distance myself from it. Now it's a journey I hold close. It's by doing this that I've learnt to find self-acceptance and 'forgiveness' (for an experience that society paints as our fault, when it is anything but that). In my good moments, I'm proud of that journey and I love the parts of me that grew out of depression.

Twelve years on from that first panic attack (aged 36 to my then 24-year-old self), I've weathered seven encounters with depression (between three and ten months long), countless doctor appointments, more psychiatric drugs than I ever wanted, bucket loads of hurt and confusion, and the loss of my confidence and self-compassion. Depression, and my meandering path of self-discovery since, has changed me forever. There's nothing I've done in life that has felt harder.

I believe that the hardest thing about depression isn't just living with it, or the painful process of climbing out of that hole, but everything that surrounds it. Trying to stay well, dealing with the shame and guilt stemming from deep societal misunderstanding, grappling with our identity in the aftermath, coping with a diagnosis which we may or may not find helpful, picking up the pieces of our shattered confidence – all this and more. A mental health journey is so much more than just the mental health struggles themselves.

I'm still working all of this out – so if you are, too, we're in the same boat. I wouldn't be the person I am, living the life I am today, without my first therapist. I first stepped into her office 12 years ago, right at the end of depression visit number one. From that day forth, my life did a handbreak turn round a switch-back corner and chartered a new course. I've now had two hugely influential therapists in my life; therapy has been, and continues to be, instrumental on my path forward.

The right support from the right people can be completely transformative through the twists and turns of a mental health journey. It might come from a therapist, or from friends, family or anyone else in your 'support crew'. None of us have to do this alone. We all deserve support.

So, how did depression come stomping into my life, bringing its havoc in tow? I don't believe there are always clear-cut answers. The only certainty is that no one has perfect mental health.

I have my own 'quirks' (or unique 'differences') that probably played into that first depressive breakdown. I grew up an easy-going, but 'perfectionist' kid and young adult. Always pushing to attain the best grades, playing on every sports team imaginable and trying to be an exemplary friend and daughter, I was – and still am – the type who would set their personal expectations 'silly high'. Characters like me can be perfect fodder for dips in mood – failing to meet the lofty standards we set can create a very real sense of failure. Depending on factors unique to the individual – including temperament and life experiences – that could (but doesn't always) spiral into depression.

Around the time of my first, and most severe, depressive episode, I was also coming to terms with my sexuality as a queer woman. While I wasn't 'out', I felt I was leading a double life, lying about where I was and who I was with. Society can apply an undeniably soul-crushing pressure to minority groups, cultivating discrimination, abuse and even self-directed prejudice (e.g. internalized homophobia). There's a reason why incidences of mental health issues, and specifically self-harm and suicide, are statistically higher among the LGBTQIA+ (lesbian, gay, bisexual, transgender, queer, intersex, asexual and others) community.

There is more to my story than my mental health journey. I'm an exercise and fitness fanatic (a key coping mechanism in my many recoveries) and adore being a spinning instructor in my spare time. I love food and cooking (my favourite meal: a smoked salmon and cream cheese bagel, shared with my family). I'd go to a live music gig every week if I could, I have seven tattoos (I always said I'd never get a single one) and I'm a loving and loyal daughter, sister and friend. I'm more than just a 'depression' diagnosis (we all are) and there's greater nuance and complexity to the challenges I've encountered than that which I've shared so far.

All of this will come out in the stories that are woven into the thoughts, advice and illustrations I share. For now, I want to leave you with my motivation to write and illustrate this book.

Something happened after first 'doing time' with depression, and the recovery that followed. I felt a red thread run between me and every other person I met who had been depressed. I was part of a vast network of people who, to some degree, were like me; I could feel that current of connection running through me, as real as anything. To hear their stories made my eyes sting with tears and my heart feel heavy. When they told me of the difficulty of just making it through the day, I felt I could reach out and touch their pain. All I've ever wanted to do since is to talk openly about depression, help people kick it to the curb and, most importantly, to love themselves throughout.

It took many years of therapy – and lots of my own reading – to one day join the dots. I had nurtured the belief that we all have the power to look after our own mental health – and, in fact, only we can lead our own recovery. I'd also picked up the tools, knowledge and confidence I needed to believe I could help myself and, importantly, others. In these pages, I hope to do what I wish someone could have done for me – helped empower me to feel more confident, more accepting of myself and less held back by fear.

Jacs the Badass Mental Health Master and her Pet Hope

I've learnt that this is a never-ending journey. Some days, I'm terrified by a possible Depression Comeback Tour, and on others I feel as if I could train up a swarm of depression-busting ninjas. That is the complexity of mental health and the fragility of confidence, especially once it's been through the depression mill. But, if we can build on that self-belief, even just a little, that is magical and powerful. This is where I am today on my mental health journey, so I'm right here with you as we navigate our onward paths.

There is no single way to give depression the sucker punch it so deeply deserves. In this book, I share tips, tools, personal stories and lessons learnt that I hope might help you, wherever you are on your very own journey. Giving depression a slap around the chops is, to me, only part of the story, however. Nurturing our self-compassion, self-belief, and love for ourselves – in spite of depression – is going to form a huge part of this road we walk together. Depression isn't something to be ashamed of, it does not make you a 'lesser' human being, and we have every right to feel proud of ourselves.

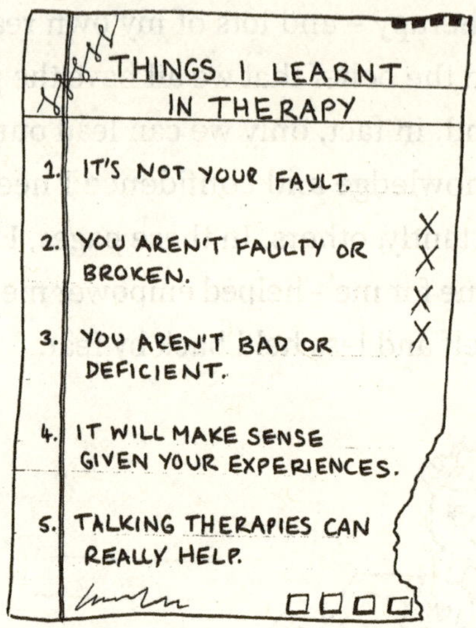

Why an illustrated self-help book? Is it for me?

Self-help books invite their fair share of sceptics. Yet, there is plenty of evidence that they can be effective in addressing mental health concerns, and even more so when combined with therapy. Unfortunately, therapy isn't accessible to all, so I wrote this book to help in its own right and in its own way. Of course, it also has the added bonus of being totally bullshit-free! I'm sharing the knowledge I've gained through my many messy dealings with depression, and using that to bring you something real.

But why all the drawings? It's not just because I like to draw. Many therapists use a range of visual elements in therapy – diagrams, flow-charts, mind-maps, and more – to explore helpful concepts. I hope that my illustrations might serve a similar purpose; they take key ideas – on what maintains our low mood and how we can manage that – and turn them into easily digestible visual prompts. Some of my drawings are simply there to be a bit comical or slightly silly – I like to think that's the beauty of how I choose to talk about my mental health and tell my story. Everything washes down better with a touch of silliness and it's nice to find moments of levity among the tough stuff. I hope that, in your lowest moment, you might remember that drawing of a box of floss, a cloud in a Hercules skirt, or an ice cream in a cape (I promise these will make sense later) and be reminded that you are not powerless against depression.

If you are seeking support for your mental health, or supporting someone else who needs it, this book is for you, and even more so if you haven't been able to access therapy. We all know if we're 'not feeling quite right' (and I don't believe we need a medical diagnosis to prove this). If you think your mental health could be in a better place than it is, you deserve support – and I hope this book can be part of yours.

What will 'feeling better' look like?

Franklin D. Roosevelt's quote, 'a smooth sea never made a skilled sailor',[1] is my first therapist's favourite saying. In her words, the quote reflects that a life with no challenges, no obstacles and no setbacks doesn't give us the skills to overcome later turbulence. She used it as a phrase to represent recovery, which often feels like taking 'two steps forward and one step back'. Or, as I prefer to say, like being stranded at sea and caught in a cyclone, which will have you turned upside down and back to front, forgetting your own name, and never knowing when it'll let up.

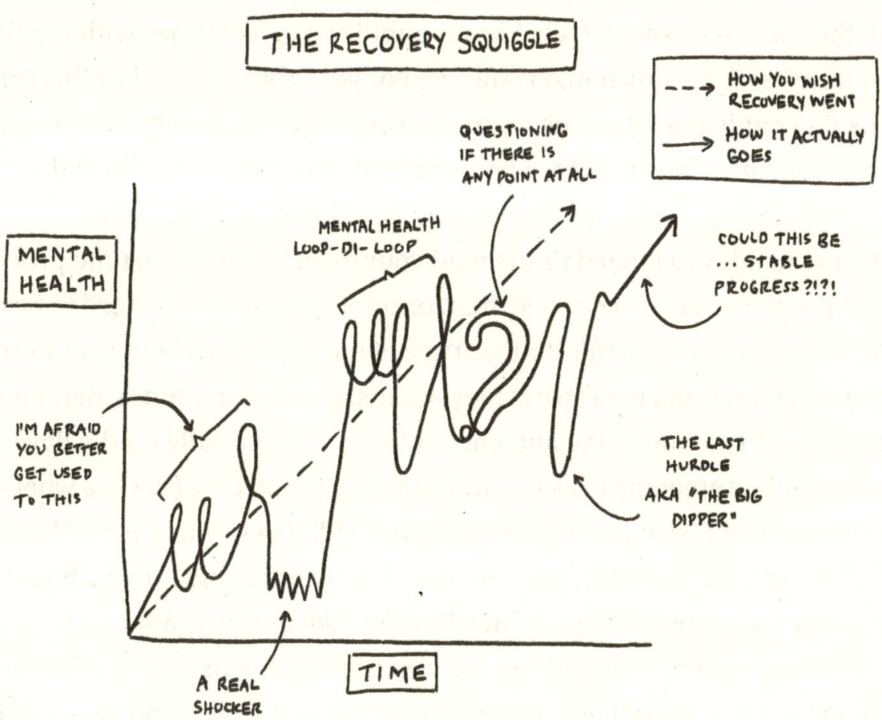

Recovery is rarely linear – in fact, you could say that the idea of a 'linear recovery' is a myth. It's so important that all discussions around our mental health, and pulling ourselves out of a depression hole, start with this idea. My therapist had met countless people, making great progress, ready to throw in the towel after a bad day, a negative interaction or a torrent of destructive thoughts. To return to my earlier nautical theme, it is these challenges (waves) and setbacks (currents) that will develop our skills in steering our boat to recovery, or wherever we're aiming for. I know that I am able to withstand more precisely because of everything I've withstood so far.

'Feeling better' might look like things returning to how you used to feel before depression swooped in or it could look a little different, perhaps intentionally so (either is valid and it depends on our circumstances). As individuals, our end goals will be diverse and the routes to reaching them unpredictable, with squiggles and bumps along the way. So, if your journey feels a little 'up and down', don't worry – embracing the squiggle is all part of the plan.

How do I know it'll work?

When the road to recovery feels like an uphill struggle, strewn with a million booby traps, and the finish line is the start of yet another race, but this time – surprise! – your legs are tied, how can you trust that my advice will work? And, how will you know it's working, when depression's tagline is 'You're failing and shit?' After all, depression is its name and hopelessness is its game.

On one hand, you'll need to suspend your disbelief and 'trust the process'. Signs of progress may feel non-existent, or miniscule, and we'll need to be persistent and patient as we wait for the fruits of our labour to show. On the other hand, we can track and measure achievements, so we notice those incremental changes – in turn, motivating and encouraging us, especially on the days that we feel ourselves creeping back towards our depression cave (the one where we sit on the sofa and wish the day away). Think of it like training for a 5km race (if you can bear the thought); you'd note each of your training times, hopefully seeing your speed improve over time. We can take a similar approach.

I must reiterate that sometimes we won't notice the progress we've made. Low mood is a miserable, lying, cheating brain-drain that will convince you that you're failing today, just as you failed yesterday, and will fail again tomorrow. With practice, we can train ourselves to see the positive steps we've taken, even when depression is trying to pretend that they're unimportant or non-existent.

Rather annoyingly, depression is well practised in the art of disguise and deception. I truly realized this on receiving a text from a close friend when I was first depressed:

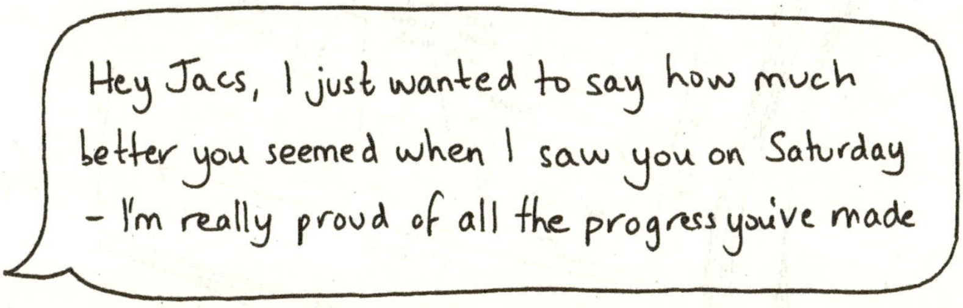

As I read those words (in a moment I remember well, as I was really leaning into depression, kneeling on the floor, head buried in my duvet cover, trying to shut out the world), a peculiar thing happened. Those words hit me like a lightning bolt – they had cut through my Depression Voice (the one that tells us we're useless, worthless, and unloveable, to name just a few) and sunk in. I believed my friend had seen something in me that I couldn't.

I stopped and thought for a moment. Did I seem better last time I saw her? I still hated myself just as much, there was no doubting that, but I think perhaps the conversation had flowed more, and I'd told her about the nice day out with my mum with genuine enthusiasm. My friend was right – I was doing more and seeming brighter. She could see the progress that I couldn't see in myself. Not only that, but here was also proof – my depressed mind was lying to me, I wasn't failing at everything.

This was a starting point. I had the beginnings of a counter-narrative that was starting to speak up in defiance. With this slim glimmer of hope, I found the foundations for a new resolve, though shaky at first. My friend's feedback really had made me feel good, so my hypothesis was that I could do the same for myself, off my own back. Noticing my own progress had never felt easy, but the more I invested in noticing it, the more I could drown out the Depression Voice and spur myself on to make more positive changes.

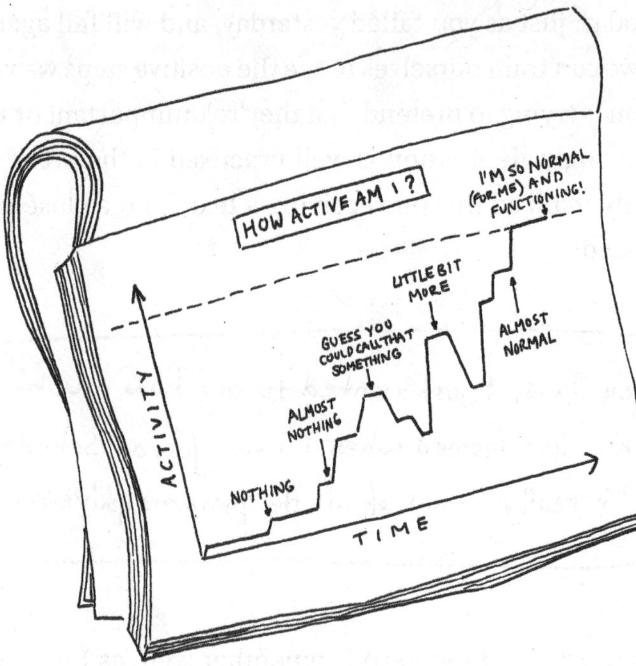

That's what I'm going to ask you to do, as you move through the stories, concepts and advice in this book. Be the friend that you deserve, attuned to, and proud of, the steps you're taking – whether they're confident strides or wobbly, tentative steps for now. The first challenge is to acknowledge that positive action, however big or small. You may find it helpful to briefly note the steps down. That way, you can look back on them and remind yourself of how well you're doing on the days when the voice in your head is going for an A+ in confidence-crushing criticism.

What might that look like? Here's how it played out for me, mid-depression.

October 2021

Mum and I went on a weekend away, to the coast, while I was still depressed. I was only open to it because I remembered that the last time I'd recovered from depression, it had started with a family trip to Ireland that I'd been dreading. I was hoping this trip might be good for me.

As soon as we arrived, I felt a weight lift. Going out to dinner

– something which I'd not managed recently without days of anticipatory dread – wasn't totally awful. It was sort of enjoyable, in fact. It was in a quiet, apprehensive way, as I trialled this old friend called 'joy' once more, but it felt positive nonetheless. It was such a significant moment that I still remember exactly what I ordered (scampi and chips).

'I'm sure this is an improvement on how I've been', I thought to myself, 'Maybe I could try and keep this up when I get home.'

Arriving home, I messaged my friend, Tash, and arranged to play tennis with her. Initiating seeing a friend was unheard of behaviour for the past ten months – I made another mental note.

A week later, it was my birthday and friends were asking me if we could go out to celebrate (Depression Voice: 'They're pretending – there's not a single thing worth celebrating about you'). This felt big, as the most socially courageous thing I'd managed recently was that tennis match. Still, I took a deep breath, and replied, 'I'd love to' to a few friends. I had three social plans in one week in my diary. The idea still felt anxiety-inducing, but less so than before, thanks to my trip away with Mum and that tennis match with Tash.

From there, things felt different. October passed by with a new gentleness, free from the constant fear of the next friend I'd have to turn down seeing. I was tentatively embracing social arrangements and felt almost like a non-depressed person! The truth is that, by this point, I was barely depressed.

With each new milestone I hit – going out in a group rather than one-on-one; running outside rather than hiding away doing home workouts; reaching out to a friend whom I'd ignored – I thought, 'Gosh, last week I couldn't do this', and now I was leaping into each new challenge I set myself.

I barely recognized this person. Surveying my progress, it dawned on me: I'd very nearly recovered and I wouldn't be stopping until I had. Two weeks later I was free from depression.

This review wasn't a formal, structured assessment, and it doesn't need to be. Most of the time I carried out this 'progress audit', I wasn't aware I was doing it. The Depression Voice still told me that I was useless, albeit in a quieter way. But I'd started in motion a slow, steady change, and later it took off in a whoosh and there I was, careering towards 'okay mental health'. I could feel a new drive. The more signs I had of progress, the more aware I became of a gentle momentum bubbling away, and the more it felt natural to keep pushing myself, in whatever way felt manageable.

There will still be days when we feel we haven't made any progress. This is one of depression's favourite lies, which we'll come to explore in more detail. However, let's assume for a moment that it's true. You're allowed to stay in one place, when you need to, and rest can be productive. Depression can feel so very debilitating and some days we simply won't feel we can push ourselves. There will also be days and weeks when we're sure that we've gone backwards. Perhaps you cancelled on a friend, when yesterday you'd been taken aback by how you'd breezed into a social outing. Some days, the very fact that the only jumper we felt confident in is unexpectedly in the wash could be enough to send us spiralling, feeling unable to venture out as planned. This is normal, we're humans – with fluctuations in mood, energy, self-belief and confidence – not machines.

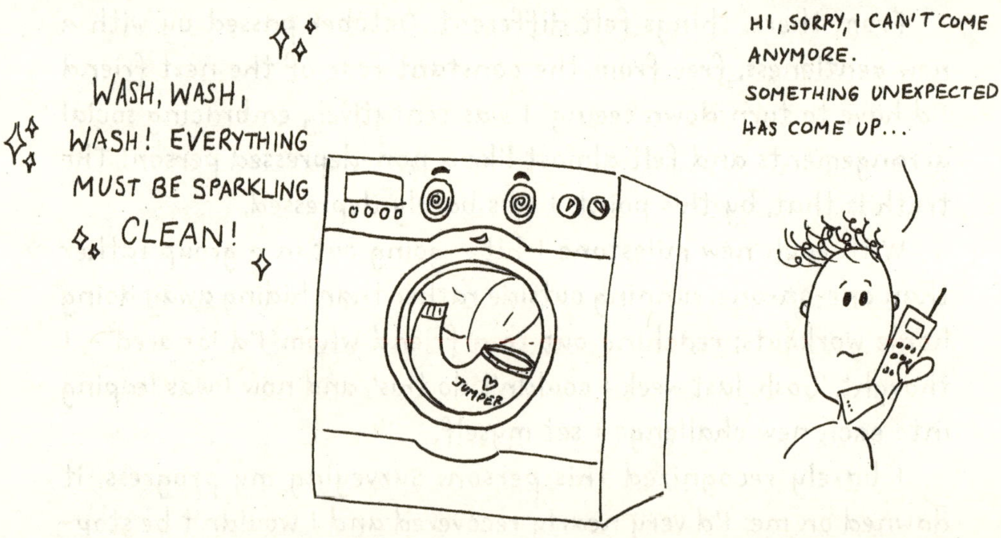

One step back doesn't permanently undo our progress, nor take us back to square one. It's in these moments that it's useful for us to review our recent achievements (kept in a note on our phone, perhaps), to remind ourselves of this. We can practise self-compassion and understanding: 'If I've managed to get to the gym every week for the past three weeks, today was just a blip, and I'll go next week instead.' Knowing we can have good and bad days along the way helps us keep going when we might feel like giving up. We're compiling a database of evidence – and looking for trends across time, rather than discreet incidences – that not even depression can argue with (and we all know how stubborn it is).

The road to recovery is never linear. We can hold this knowledge in mind, while assessing our progress, to remember that, among all the ups and downs and inevitably difficult emotions, we're still travelling in the right direction. We can keep moving, keep noticing the incremental steps along the way, and one day we'll be looking back, unable to believe just how far we have come.

What to expect

This book does not contain sure-fire answers to navigating a life that depression has decided to gatecrash; no one can claim to have those. But what this book does have is a whole bunch of practical tips and advice, woven around a generous helping of illustrations (sometimes making it easier to visualize an important concept; other times, for a bit of silly fun), to encourage you to explore an approach to managing your mental health that might just work for you. Through my own lived experience of depression and recovery – from the 'aha!' moments to the flailing around in the dark – I'll be offering a starting point from which to embark on your own journey of 'trial and error' (because that's key in all of this). It's combined with many of the lessons I learnt in therapy, taken from the field of psychology and firmly rooted in well-known psychological theories.

I truly believe we can all take a proactive role in our recovery. So, we'll learn how depression works and what feeds it, alongside making a plan that uses that knowledge to undermine depression's supposed power and gradually chip away at low mood. Understanding the role of our support networks will be central in pulling it all together – with advice for your biggest cheerleaders included (and help on where to find them). Lastly, and perhaps most crucially, we're going to pay attention to the person behind the mental health experience: you. Depression leaves its mark on our lives in so many ways – long after the damn thing ever showed up and got its business everywhere – and I know for a fact that we can all do with a good dose of self-love and confidence along the way. Sometimes we just need a bit of help finding it.

With that, it's time to get started.

* **CHAPTER 2** *

The Psychology to Make Sense of it All

What does depression look and feel like?

Depression and low mood radically alter the way that we see and interpret the world.

Nothing about the world has changed. There is still room for beauty, joy and silliness, just as there is space for sadness, anger and hurt. Yet, depression manages to strip the world of this balance, removing any equilibrium, and tipping the scale in favour of the negative. In a world where light and dark exist in beautiful yet chaotic harmony, depression shuts out the light and allows darkness to flood in.

This one-dimensional perspective, where everything is reduced to the negative, lowers our mood, which in turn changes our thoughts and behaviours and feeds back into that negative cycle (we'll look at why this is in the next section). It is a question of perspective shift – not a change in reality – but one that we can feel powerless to control.

Of course, challenging life events happen, and these can feel as if they've altered life's very foundations – loss, breakups, abuse, illness, injustice, financial struggle, and much more, will do that. While the world may not have changed in material terms (it still has the same potential for good and bad as ever), your circumstances have, and your perception of change is enough to trigger that dip in mood. Sometimes, it may seem as if nothing has changed to cause this shift, yet you still feel the crushing weight of low mood. There doesn't need to be an obvious or justifiable reason to be feeling low. How you feel is valid regardless of how you perceive your situation.

In short, our perceptions can feel like reality, and affect us as though they were real, even though they may not be. Depression capitalizes on this to persuade us that life is 'just shit' and so our mood drops.

Now, to get to know what we're dealing with, I'm about to plunge us into the depths of depression. Warning: things are about to get rather dark, as I introduce you to a depressed Jacs. It's not pretty, but it'll only be for a moment.

A day in the life of a depressed Jacs

You wake up. Your bedroom wall that you first lay your eyes on, the one with the piece of art on it that you once loved, feels overwhelmingly awful. How can a *wall* remind you of how each minute of your day has become a painful crawl towards the end of your disappointing life? And who the hell chose that tasteless painting?

When you finally get out of bed, you feel flat. As if a depression steamroller has done its business all over you, being careful to really flatten out that self-esteem, self-confidence and self-worth, until you've forgotten who you are. Reduced to a paper-thin version of yourself, your emotions, capacity to love, and hope, have all been compressed into virtual non-existence. Today feels colourless and empty, just like every other day.

You look in the mirror: ugly, so ugly.

Now your daily pep-talk has been carried out with your usual aplomb, it's time to get dressed. What combination of the hideous clothes in your wardrobe says, 'I'm the worst human being you'll meet today, steer the hell clear of me'?

You're too repulsive to leave the house today (and every day), so, same old unwashed khaki t-shirt again it is. Don't even mention the 'shower' word – not a chance.

As you dress, you wonder how it got to this – where everything you liked about yourself has been lost, leaving you with the very worst of your traits (selfish, self-involved) and inheriting some new, equally disappointing ones (reclusive, lazy, unkind). While we're on the topic, where the hell did you pick those up? You've barely been out the house or seen a soul for months, apart from your family (who you are treating like poop on the bottom of your shoe). You really must have mined the depths of your depressed soul to find these new shockers. Typical you; the only thing you excel at is becoming an even worse human being than you already were.

You would feel upset about this 'new you' except this is just what you're like now. There's no point fighting it – everything is hopeless, anyway. You are hopeless, you are worthless, you are a pathetic failure, and a better person wouldn't be here.

Being honest, you wish you weren't.

Depression is unforgiving and unrelenting in its pursuit of making you feel as awful as possible about yourself. Meanwhile, it will try to convince you that it doesn't even exist, that it all comes from you. It's sly like that.

This is our Depression Voice, and it will keep on at you, making you feel small, meek and 'lesser than'. It makes me want to hide away (so I do), to tread on this earth apologetically, disgusted by myself, ashamed of the hurt I'm bringing others and the space I'm taking up that I don't feel I deserve.

On its worst days, that voice will hold a distorted mirror up to you that shows you your new 'truth' (though, based on lies and fabrication): you're the worst type of human being there is, the type that doesn't deserve to exist. Throw on top of that some hardcore shame. 'How did you let yourself get like that?' it chides, while protesting, 'Don't look at me, it's got nothing to do with me.'

This is a depressed mind when low mood has us caught in its grip and we're unable to see our true worth. Thankfully, many of us won't stay at the very bottom of this gloomy pit. Little by little, its hold tires and weakens, and the 'old you' starts to appear through the gaps in its dull, shabby exterior. Faint, shimmering shafts of light creep through in fragile slivers, casting a glow on the best parts of you that you'd forgotten ever existed. I once asked my therapist if I could ever completely lose the 'real me' because of depression. She replied, 'Depression feels like a cloak that casts a dark shadow over us and obscures all the beautiful parts of you. But, when depression begins to lift, so too will that cloak, and you will be reintroduced to the vibrant, full-colour version of yourself.' That's the light flooding back in, restoring true colour to a world of grey.

It doesn't stay dark forever. The tough bit is that it feels as if that darkness is everlasting when you're in the thick of it. We're here to learn how we can stand strong against that feeling, challenging it until it dissipates.

Through my 'journal entry', you saw a glimpse of what my depression looks like, but it won't look or feel the same for any two people. Some will be able to go on 'functioning' – for example, working and seeing friends – while their pain is carefully and purposefully hidden. Others' lives will grind to a halt, and they are barely able to get out of bed or have a conversation. Some will turn to behaviours that will feel like 'coping strategies', such as alcohol and drug abuse, or self-harm. This can confuse outsiders with certain preconceived notions about what depression should, or does, look like.

Our low mood exists on a spectrum: there have been times when I've been able to continue working and just about leaving the house, and times when I haven't. It is important to stress that your feelings, and how they present, are yours and yours alone. No one can tell you if they 'look like depression' (not even the doctor who told me that I didn't look depressed – thanks, Doc). There is no hierarchy of suffering. As my first therapist once said to me, 'Your pain is your pain – we are entitled to recognize and own our feelings, no matter how they compare to others.'

I have learnt that to accept ourselves *with* our depression (which I believe is essential), we have to get to know it and show compassion towards the depressed 'us'. You don't have to become best buddies with your depression, but you know what they say about keeping your enemies close... We're on a new mission – becoming acquaintances with our depression, right before slaying it.

Life really can get back to a better place – whether that's how things were before or simply better than now (recovery doesn't always have to mean getting back to exactly where we were – it might or we may have adapted goals that better suit our circumstances). When my mood has lifted, the world hasn't changed but my perceptions have. I can feel the love in my mum's hugs again, appreciate the blowing kisses emoji at the end of a best friend's text, and truly savour a simple walk in the sun. But, most importantly, I know that I'm a good, kind, loving daughter, sister and friend. These are my truths, not what depression would have me believe, and we *can* get back to our own reality.

Of course I wasn't the worst person to have graced this earth when I was depressed. But I can now challenge the belief that 'a better person wouldn't be here [down a dingy depression hole]'. I didn't get depressed because I'm terrible; I felt terrible *because I was depressed* – this is such a crucial distinction to hold on to.

* * *

So now we know, depression lies and those lies are dangerous and skew our perceptions of ourselves. This is one of the most crucial pieces of knowledge we can use to rugby tackle depression to the floor. Soon, we'll be learning how we can challenge depression's bullshit till it realizes it's been caught out and gives in.

I want to start by challenging depression's fake 'truths' (or 'bullshit', to use a technical term) right now. You are not an awful person for having been through depression – not during or after it. Depression is indescribably hard to navigate, and you're simply brilliant for having weathered the storm.

Understanding suicide and depression

I remember the first time I tried to tell my therapist that I'd felt suicidal. I sat there, lump in my throat, adrenaline coursing, feeling as if all that would come out, if I tried to say it, was a croaky noise, like a weird frog admitting to their darkest thoughts. It felt too big an admission, too serious, too unusual. When I plucked up the courage to admit that I had felt suicidal, my therapist didn't so much as stir in response to something she'd heard many times before. While I would never claim that feeling suicidal is normal – a feeling that comes from the deepest pit of human pain isn't something I wish to normalize – it is not uncommon.

Depression is a big risk factor for suicide, but not all people who are suicidal are depressed and not everyone who is depressed will be suicidal. That said, the thoughts and feelings that come along with feeling suicidal are the kinds of thoughts that we might experience when we're feeling extremely low or depressed. However, they'll have become loud enough and persistent enough that the person experiencing them cannot see a more rational and truthful interpretation of their circumstances and their position in this world. It is in this way that they might believe that the best, or only, option is to take their own life.

However, I really want to stress that it doesn't have to mean the end of the road if you, or someone you know, has thoughts of suicide. There is often a way through it, and many people experience it and survive it – eventually getting to a place where they no longer want to end their life. There are professionals out there who can help you and ways you can support someone, and it is vital that anyone who is experiencing suicidal ideation (thinking about or planning for suicide), or is feeling suicidal, is provided with the right support (my website has details of support groups; more details are in the back of the book).

If you're feeling suicidal, the very best thing you can do, however hard it feels, is to tell someone. You're wanted on this earth, and you deserve support.

Struggle with the term 'depression'?

You're talking to the Mayor of Struggle Town, when it comes to trying to feel comfortable with the word 'depression'. It can be a tricky word for many, myself included. I dislike the thought of anyone being given a label that doesn't resonate with them – plus, many of us didn't ask for a label at all. The likelihood is that we went to our doctor, feeling low and unsure what to do, and we left with a 'depression' diagnosis (and maybe even a couple of others, like 'anxiety', for good measure) and a prescription for anti-depressants. It makes sense that this feels uncomfortable to some. Meanwhile, for others, having a recognized diagnosis feels reassuring – it explains why things have been the way they have, and it gives a clear way to communicate that.

Identity, and using language that we feel accurately represents our lived experience, is so important. If you don't feel that a word matches your internal sense of self, you shouldn't have to use it – and you don't. After all, if a bunch of psychiatrists can gather in a room, put together a diagnostic manual, and fill it with made up names for new 'mental health conditions' or 'illnesses', based on groupings of symptoms alone (because there isn't a single medical test in existence that can prove the presence of a 'mental illness'), then I do believe we are at liberty to make up our own names too!

My first therapist always encouraged me to call it whatever I wanted: low mood, fug, depression, blues, the dark times and infinite others. If you don't feel comfortable with the term 'depression', here's a list of names that my therapist had come across in her time – feel free to pick one, or many! It really is your decision. Cloud, misery, low mood, unhappiness, distress, fog, fug, slump, blue mood, despondency, feeling crap, feeling shit, hopelessness, gloom, doom, dysthymia, melancholy, unhappiness, dejection, mental pain, woes and gloom.

The descriptor itself really doesn't matter – I started out calling my depression the 'dark times'. It is only important that whatever we choose to call it feels comfortable (sometimes that might just be the least awful option of a bad bunch). While I struggled with calling my 'thing' depression, my therapist was adamant that I didn't let my name for it, or lack thereof, prevent me from acknowledging my struggles and getting the support I needed – whether that was the love and care of my friends or anti-depressants from the doctor. Giving that 'thing' a name of any kind is useful because it can validate a really horrible, and even traumatic, experience, helping us believe that support is deserved. Whatever language we choose – even if we don't have the words for it – we all deserve solutions if we don't feel right.

The cognitive model: Your key to understanding negative thought patterns

Now, here comes the science.

All of our difficulties have a number of factors. These are aspects of our lives and our experiences which, in good times, work to support each other, but at difficult times can exacerbate our difficulties.

* **Environment:** People, places, events.
* **Thoughts/interpretations:** What goes through your mind when something happens? What we think a recent event says about us, what we assume others are thinking, or what we imagine will happen next.
* **Moods:** How we feel in ourselves – whether we feel cheerful, sad, angry, fearful and so on.
* **Behaviours:** What we do as a result of how we feel, something that happens, or a thought we have. It can be a physical response (like keeping our head down and not looking at people), or something we don't do (like not going out or not picking up the phone when it rings), or something we regret (like ending a relationship because we believe we're not good enough).
* **Physical reactions:** The ways in which our bodies react to whatever is going on. For example, feeling physically exhausted when our mood is low, or having a bad stomach from anxiety.

These factors are all linked and affect each other. By understanding the way they relate, we can begin to work out how small changes in one factor can have a knock-on effect on others. The theory is that we should be able to improve many areas of difficulty by concentrating our efforts on one or two factors.

The way we think about events or experiences affects the way that we feel (our mood), the way our bodies function (our physical reactions) and what we do (our behaviour). These, in turn, affect our environment. For example, if we stop going out, we can lose contact with friends and have fewer people around to help us cope with our difficulties.

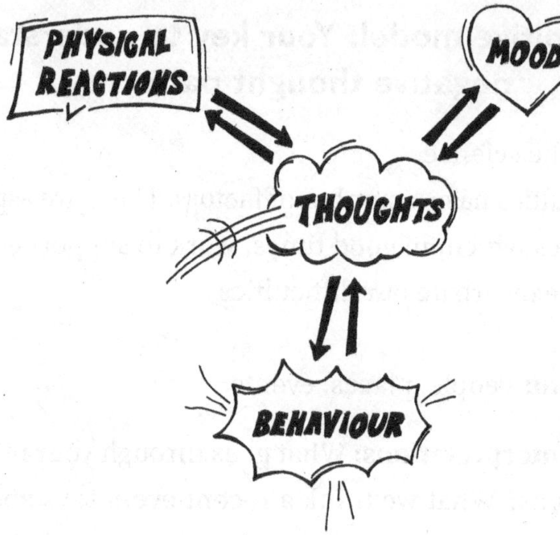

These areas of our functioning continue to affect each other in a loop. For example, once our mood is low, this affects the way we think. Suppose you're walking down the street, and you see a friend who appears to ignore you completely. You might wonder why they've turned against you and feel sad/embarrassed/hurt. Later, you mention the incident to that friend, who tells you they were preoccupied at the time and didn't even see you. Normally, you would feel better and put what happened out of your mind. When depressed, you are more likely to believe that your friend intentionally ignored you and feel rejected. You may not even ask them about the incident, so the mistake goes unexplained. When low or depressed, you're more likely to make assumptions or draw biased conclusions like this repeatedly. A recipe for feeling even more miserable, I'm sure you'll agree.

Once our mood is lowered, it affects the way we process information in three ways. First, we tend to notice all the negative things that happen around us, rather than the positive things, and can find ourselves looking out for more 'bad' things. Second, we tend to remember all the bad things that have happened to us and forget that we have had positive experiences. For example, we might remember the one negative piece of feedback at work, and forget all our professional achievements that year. Finally, we tend to interpret our experiences in the most negative way possible, just like the incident with our friend who accidentally ignored us. I like to visualize this skewed perspective as viewing the world through a pair of 'low mood specs'.

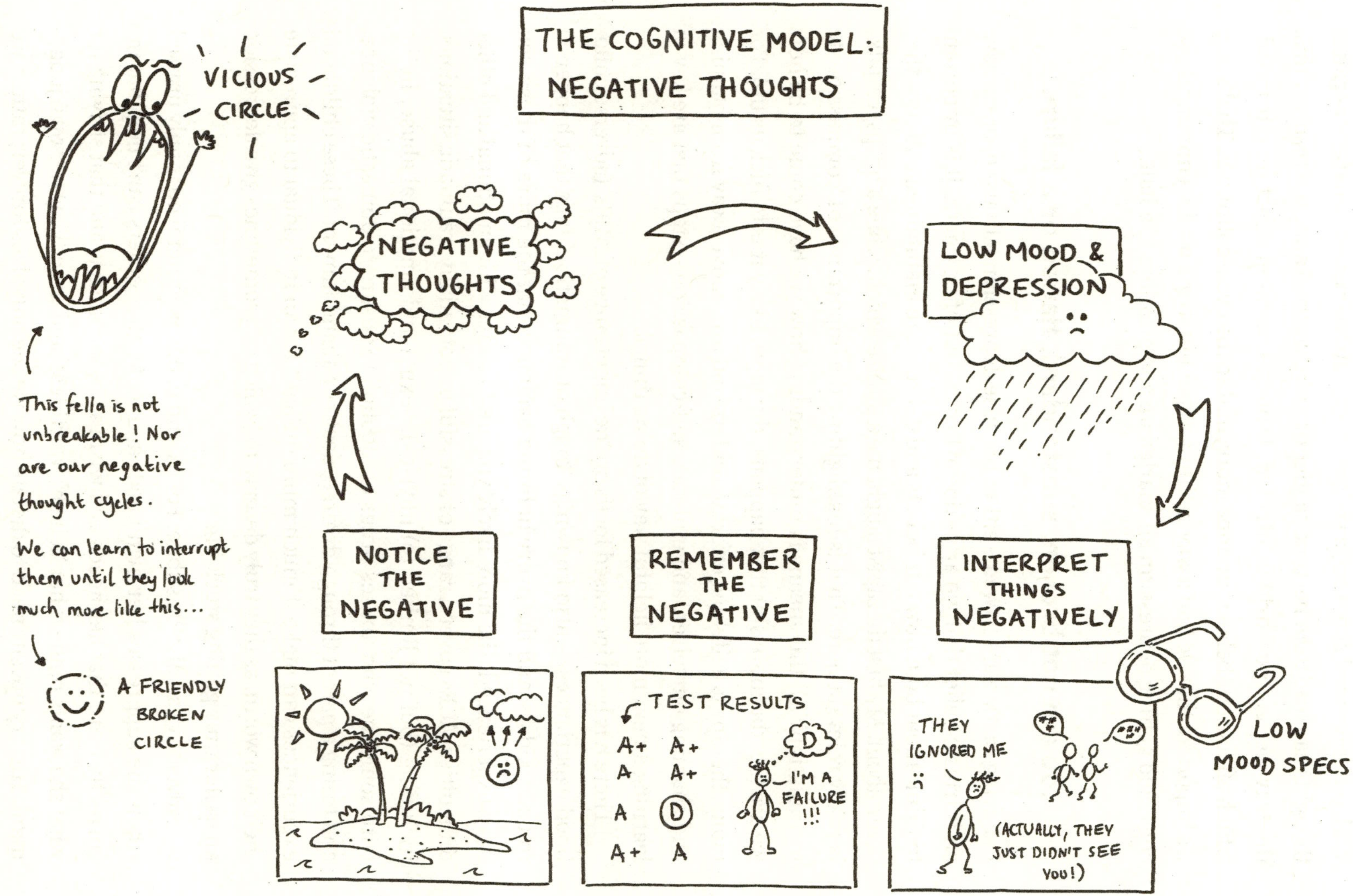
THE COGNITIVE MODEL:
NEGATIVE THOUGHTS
VICIOUS CIRCLE
This fella is not unbreakable! Nor are our negative thought cycles.
We can learn to interrupt them until they look much more like this...
A FRIENDLY BROKEN CIRCLE
NEGATIVE THOUGHTS
LOW MOOD & DEPRESSION
NOTICE THE NEGATIVE
REMEMBER THE NEGATIVE
INTERPRET THINGS NEGATIVELY
TEST RESULTS
A+ A+
A A+
A D
A+ A
D
I'M A FAILURE !!!
THEY IGNORED ME
(ACTUALLY, THEY JUST DIDN'T SEE YOU!)
LOW MOOD SPECS

With our low mood specs on, a vicious circle can be created, whereby negative thoughts can lead us to become sadder or more worried and, as a result of this, the way we see the world is affected. It has a knock-on effect on our mood, which affects our behaviour once more, and so the cycle continues. That's why it's important that we find a way to throw a spanner in the works, jamming those cogs, and getting depression all snarled up and grinding to a halt.

You are not broken, substandard, flawed or a failure

Believing that we are flawed – either because depression tells us so, or we have an intrinsic belief that we are – doesn't come out of nowhere. It is important to think about both how our beliefs and distress are maintained and how they come about. My first therapist taught me a phrase which, while a bit 'psych-talk', is really relevant here. That is highlighting the importance of 'compassionate formulation'. All this means is understanding how we have come to be how we are (i.e. the more shit that happens, the more likely it is to fuck us up). For many, therapy is a lifelong effort to understand this, move away from blaming and shaming ourselves, and embrace self-compassion – steps that are key in learning a new, more helpful way of doing things.

There has been increased focus on the importance of 'ACEs' (adverse childhood experiences) – also known as 'tough or traumatic things that happened to us as kids' – and the overwhelming evidence that the more of these you have experienced, the more likely you are to suffer with emotional and other difficulties. ACEs cover a range of stressful or potentially traumatic situations, including (but not limited to) physical, sexual and emotional abuse, living with someone who abuses drugs or alcohol, exposure to domestic violence, and losing a parent through divorce, death or abandonment. These childhood experiences can make it much more difficult for an individual to appreciate their own worth, as they truly deserve to (which can sometimes give depression an easier time getting stuck in).

Adversity can also be subtle. For example, the daughter who is only praised when she suppresses her own needs and looks after others can't help but incorrectly learn that her needs and wishes are secondary, and that striving for what she wants renders her 'selfish', 'worthless' and 'greedy' by her own judgement. History doesn't need to dictate how we see ourselves forever; rather, we should allow ourselves to understand why we feel as we do, while challenging it whenever we can (therapy can be great for this). It is an opportunity to show compassion for the imperfect, winding road that got us here, and acknowledge a start in life that wasn't our doing or our choosing.

Balancing chemical imbalance perspectives

There have been years of research, millions of pounds and thousands of scientists focused on trying to uncover the 'secret key' to depression and whether this is purely a result of life adversity and experience or has a basis in genetics or brain chemistry. The truth is, we still don't know what causes depression. So, different researchers with different backgrounds will claim different things. You might hear that early life trauma affects brain chemistry, that those with close relatives with a history of depression are more likely to become depressed, and you may come across debates as to whether genetics underlie this, or even whether families who share negative thinking styles might be the root cause.

Of these, there is one theory that, for many decades, has provided the dominant narrative or 'explanation' for why we get depressed: the 'chemical imbalance' theory.

The 'chemical imbalance' theory is the belief that depression is caused and maintained by insufficient levels of the neurotransmitter 'serotonin' (a chemical messenger found in our brains). This understanding of depression's cause – though not proven – is so deeply embedded in Western society that I have heard it used as an explanation for depression from just about every kind of person you might come across in life: psychiatrists, doctors, varied mental health professionals, good friends, strangers on the internet, my librarian, that guy down the pub, and many more. However, an umbrella paper (a review of multiple existing scientific reviews), published by psychologist Dr Joanna Moncrieff in 2022, should have put this supposedly 'accepted' theory to bed. In her paper, we learn that the major research on this topic shows that 'there is no convincing evidence that depression is associated with, or caused by, lower serotonin concentrations or activity'.[2] It seems that the scientific community have long been in the know, but it hasn't filtered down.

So, in actual fact, the only thing we know about the 'chemical imbalance' theory is that there is nothing to prove that it is true, and we still don't know why we get depressed.

However, this theory persists, in spite of the latest research. It is still widely believed that a depressed person wouldn't be struggling, if only they'd had more serotonin in their brains to start with! This is problematic for two reasons. The first is that a baseless theory, with no supporting evidence, has been used to inform our understanding of a mental health condition, which affects people's fundamental life experiences, and their treatment, the world over.

The second reason that this is problematic is because the 'chemical imbalance' theory propagates a belief that, as people who have taken a turn or two on the depression treadmill, our brains are faulty, deficient, lacking – and, by extension, so are we. So, I'm here to call bullshit on a theory that we are no more able to prove than my belief that someone is perpetually stealing odd socks from my washing (I promise you, they are).

It's time for a dose of realism. What do we really know about the causes of depression? We know that life circumstances play a huge role: the more difficult or 'bad' things that happen to you, the more challenges life will present. This includes, but is not limited to, being financially challenged, facing discrimination and racism, and being forced to move, marry or make changes against your will. While the jury is still out as to whether there is a biological or chemical substrate underlying how we respond to these situations, our unique temperamental differences are also factors which could affect our vulnerability or resilience.

The World Health Organization (WHO) states that 'depression results from a complex interaction of social, psychological and biological factors',[3] also known as 'biopsychosocial' factors. Regardless of where you stand in the 'nature vs. nurture' debate, it is clear that difficult life events challenge our view of ourselves, the world and others. In turn, this changes the perspective with which we view our life, events, successes and challenges.

We may not know with certainty the cause of depression in our lifetime. I believe that what is more important is to understand why we think we might have experienced it, and look to the future – what are we able to do to lift our mood and make improvements in our lives?

Sitting and waiting

I truly believe that we can all do something to look after, and improve, our mental health. This has been one of the most empowering realizations I've had on my journey. Of course, we won't always feel ready, or able, to spring into action with our toolkit of coping strategies, and we will come on to how to navigate that scenario. For now, an important reminder: we're not super-human and no one is expecting you to be either!

Let's revisit that 'chemical imbalance' theory. It tells us that there is something intrinsically 'wrong' with our brain (i.e. that we have an imbalance of neurotransmitters, such as serotonin), which can make us feel 'broken' or 'damaged'. If we're told that medication is required to 'fix' the imbalance, it can feel as if our own agency is superseded by the purported power of a bottle of pills and a psychiatrist's prescription. If our own sense of personal control feels compromised, sitting and waiting for the medication to work is an understandable reaction, and one many of us will lean towards. I certainly have.

In 2012, when I was first given a diagnosis and a pill to swallow to 'cure' my depression, I took it. Then I waited. In the Western world, we have so much faith in medicine that the idea that it could make our depression disappear in a puff of smoke isn't a difficult one to buy into – but it is very rarely true in isolation.

There is nothing wrong with believing in the medical model (the view that mental disorders are 'disorders' or 'diseases' with biological causes) or relying on psychiatric drugs to help us along our journey. For many, they are a magical lifeline. A medical diagnosis and a pill to target its symptoms can feel deeply comforting. Having an explanation for thoughts and behaviours which have always seemed inexplicable, and often troubling, can be a huge relief, and the drugs can be effective. It can feel like hope when all had seemed hopeless.

My experience was a little different. Fresh off the back of my first panic attack, I refused to believe I had a 'mental illness', as doctors told me. I only took the anti-depressants I was prescribed because I felt I owed it to my parents. I thought I was putting them through hell, not least because I'd secretly called an ambulance out to their house three times in two days, so convinced I was that my panic attacks were in fact death coming a-knocking at my door (in the ambulance, I even told my mum, 'This is my final breath', as I dramatically clutched at her arm... It wasn't).

I couldn't have been less engaged with my treatment. Still, I was told that I needed to wait for the drugs to kick in to start to feel like the 'real me' again. So, I sat and waited – literally, I barely moved from my parents' sofa for five months.

In the years that followed this first 'breakdown', aged 24, where I was plummeted into the deepest depression I've still ever known, I was prescribed seven different psychiatric drugs. Four anti-depressants, one anxiolytic, one mood-stabilizer and one anti-psychotic drug – all handed out after fleeting appointments with six different health professionals over five years.

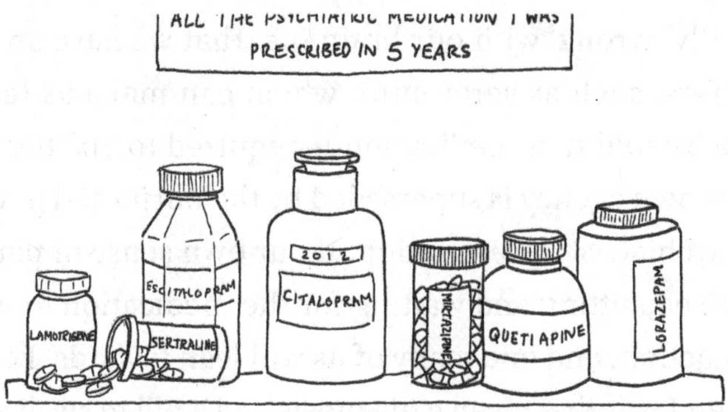

There must have been a part of me that hoped I could leave the 'healing' to the drugs. Similarly, placing my future mental well-being in the hands of a qualified professional felt sensible – and, being honest, also easier. My depression would tell me it was all my fault, that this was just how I was now, but I wanted nothing more than for someone to take it away from me and make it all better – perhaps the doctors could? I see this as an understandable response to tackling a murky topic; the work to get through depression is, first, often unclear, and, second, really hard.

What did I gain from all those years spent believing that I could do nothing about my own mental health?

In my experience, 'waiting' only provided more uncertainty for the future and a severe lack of self-belief. Once recovered, I felt I owed it to the drugs. I felt dependent on those little pills I'd swallowed every day, rather than acknowledging the hard work I'd done to get myself feeling better. Once I came off them, and I struggled with my mental health again some months later, I had no trust in my own depression-defying tools. I took more pills and waited again. I still believed myself powerless to the whims of my seemingly unpredictable mental health.

This is my story and an approach that I gradually learnt to unpick and mould into something that now feels right to me. I have decided not to take anti-depressants (though I support anyone who finds them helpful) and focus instead on learning more about my depression. There is no 'correct' way; I know people for whom an element of 'waiting until their mood lifts' feels right. There are always shades of grey, too – before I can do many of the things that contribute to my recovery, I'm starting to wonder if pausing, to some degree, is a useful or necessary precursor to a time when depression feels less all-consuming, and I feel able to be more proactive. It is all valid.

Anti-depressants, and other psychiatric drugs, are an extremely helpful form of treatment for many, and I'm pleased for anyone whose life they have improved. I've found them helpful at times, too; they've given me a feeling of safety I might not have got elsewhere. However, a drug prescription on its own is not typically the most effective form of long-term treatment. That comes from any combination of drugs, talking therapy and other practices that are good for our well-being (e.g. exercise, socializing, a healthy diet). Many studies prove that drugs in isolation may be no more effective than a placebo[4] and long-term outcomes may even be worse when taking medication.[5] Meanwhile, we can feel trapped in a cycle of jumping from one drug to the next, as we work out which are effective, or even as the drugs that previously worked seem to suddenly stop working. With this in mind, there's a case to explore the other viable options out there too.

It was the belief in the effectiveness of these alternative options and approaches – and the power I had to execute them myself, which I explored in therapy – that gave me more mental health confidence than I'd ever felt. For me, 'sitting and waiting' – and the idea that we can't do anything to improve our own situation – reinforced my feelings of hopelessness, fear and shame that depression throws in our face. The power of countering this narrative, for our future well-being and peace of mind, shouldn't be underestimated.

* * *

Fear has certainly played its fair part in the feelings that I've had to try and work through since depression first came to town. I'm not free from that fear and I'm not sure that I ever will be. However, understanding the psychology behind it all, and, from there, knowing we can play a proactive part in our recovery, has helped me regain a feeling of control that depression stole from me. It is okay, even normal, to fear depression, but we can make sure that feeling lives alongside a calm confidence in the tricks up our sleeve that'll give depression a hard time, should it dare show its face again. That's how I believe we learn to live more comfortably, and with more peace, alongside our experiences. We are not fundamentally broken, damaged or flawed – there is always a route forward.

* CHAPTER 3 *

Understanding Our Mental Health

The mental health spectrum

It's easy to feel that we're not 'depressed enough' or feeling low enough to seek support for our mental health (even when our mood is crawling on its hands and knees through the gutter). Many won't seek out the help they deserve because they believe that 'others have it worse'. I have certainly thought that how I was feeling wasn't 'bad enough' (whatever that is) to tell anyone about or to get any help. The truth is, we may not be feeling as bad as the depressed person next to us, or we may be feeling worse. It doesn't matter. Comparison shouldn't have any place in how we decide to act on our mental health. Depression has us feeling totally inadequate and unworthy, but we must try to remind ourselves that if we don't feel right, that justifies getting support.

The support will be individualized and tailored to you. If you go to a doctor, they may use a scale to rate your mood, but this isn't to make comparisons; rather, to make sure you get the right level of support for your needs. That could be talking therapy, anti-depressants, lifestyle changes, or all of the above. The most important thing is that we get the support and treatment that feels helpful and right for us. We are all important and we all deserve to feel okay.

Your depression may not look like the next person's, but that doesn't make it less valid – in fact, that is the nature of depression. Everyone's mental health exists on a spectrum and, while there may be similarities, no two people's depression will present in the same way. Some people's mood rapidly plummets to the floor (and may recover quickly again, or not), while some people feel so low for so long that they don't believe they can ever feel better again. They may have forgotten that they ever felt 'okay', instead believing that they are a defective person (when of course they are not).

Whatever your flavour of depression, we're all worthy of support to make the incremental change that could improve our life. For some, that will be managing to get out of bed, have a shower and change their clothes. For others, it might be making themselves go to after-work drinks when socializing has felt tough recently. It really is a spectrum of the broadest kind and we're all somewhere along it. Wherever you find yourself on the spectrum, and however much that changes (as it will, because that's life, with all its highs and lows), you deserve support to get you to a better place, as much as anyone else.

Depression's disguises

Given the mental health spectrum, we know that my version of depression (withdrawing, becoming quieter) may look almost nothing like someone else's (e.g. covering it up with a sunny disposition, wanting to be around others). That said, there are many shared traits of depression: social withdrawal, thoughts and behaviours that indicate low self-esteem and confidence (e.g. shying away from being seen in public, keeping quiet around others), over- or under-eating, and over-sleeping. There is also a unifying theme (or 'symptom', if you like) across everyone who is depressed: the belief that 'I am shit' (or worthless/useless/unloveable/better off dead, etc.).

However, when it comes to the *behaviours* that those depressive thoughts drive, these will differ from person to person. That's the many depression disguises for you. Your depression might come brandishing maracas, in its finest signature tropical fruit hat and pineapple sunglasses ('fun-time depression' – here for a good time, not necessarily a long time), meanwhile your friend's depression might have gone in hard with the full head-to-toe horse costume (sweaty stuff). The illustrations I've come up with are just some fun examples and they don't symbolize depression's characteristics per se; rather, the mind-blowing diversity of how it can show up and disguise itself (it really can be hard to spot). This lack of 'one size fits all' can make it hard for people, especially those who haven't experienced low mood, to accept everyone's struggles, no matter how they present.

THE MANY DEPRESSION DISGUISES

PJ PARTY DEPRESSION
- Found sleeping
- Life feels very tiring

FUN-TIME DEPRESSION
- Life and soul of the party
- Special skill: seeming happy

LONE RANGER DEPRESSION
- Prefers to go it alone
- Only needs an inflatable horse for company

SPOOKY DEPRESSION
- Spine tingling and scary
- Partial to a jump scare

HOME BODY DEPRESSION
- Found cosy-ing down at home
- Bookish! Fiction is better than reality

BRING-A-FRIEND DEPRESSION
- Always prefers company
- Likes to think 'good things come in pairs'

Take me and my friend, for example.

Last year, an old friend reached out to me because she was depressed, had temporarily moved home to live with her parents and didn't know who to turn to. We arranged to go for a coffee, but she told me that she'd rather not talk about her depression because she found she'd get 'stuck' on that topic, talking about it persistently for the rest of the conversation. I said, 'Of course', and asked her if she was okay to meet at a coffee shop, or if she would prefer somewhere quieter. She said she was happy to be out and about.

These were the unique traits of her depression – to a depressed me, this scenario would seem completely bonkers. Here's why:

* I will never tell you I'm depressed – it makes me feel too vulnerable and as though I'm attention seeking. Even if someone already knows that I'm depressed, I will not make reference to the shhh depression.
* Part of the reason for that is that I don't know that I'm depressed. Like many people's depression, mine tells big, fat, juicy lies (which we'll come on to in Chapter 11), one of which is, 'You're not depressed; you've always been this way.' I may have a hunch that I'm feeling worse than normal, but no more. It's usually only once I've bid farewell to depression that I have an 'oh fuck' moment of realization.
* Good luck trying to get me to go out in public. No thank you. I simply feel too shit about myself to be seen by, or be around, other people.

Both my friend and I had been depressed, both of us possessed a similar delightful combination of self-hatred, low self-esteem, low self-worth and lack of confidence that signal depression's tell-tale ways. Yet, our behaviour was totally different. We shared some behaviours, still, such as finding it hard to motivate ourselves to keep busy; some traits overlap, while some don't. It's a bit like a depression symptom pick 'n' mix in how they come together for an individual (though less tasty and not so bad for your teeth – just pretty horrible for the mind).

Knowing this, it's understandable that people – especially those who have never suffered from low mood or depression – might find it tricky to get their head around 'what depression looks like'. It is a confusing concept. While two people share a diagnosis (or, if without a diagnosis, similar negative thoughts about themselves and the world) they may share few of the same 'symptoms' on the surface, or they could exhibit almost identical symptoms! Don't worry – it messes with *my* mind and I've been depressed, so cut yourself, and those around you, some slack if it feels perplexing.

What's the consequence of this? First, it should inform any treatment and recovery plans we make. We need to take a flexible and open-minded approach to how we treat low mood. We've looked at some of the underlying psychology I've learnt along the way. Returning to the idea of *biopsychosocial* drivers to depression, we can approach treatment in a handful of ways that we know are likely to be helpful, based on a scientific understanding of how our brains work. Within this, the issues we tackle, the behaviours we unpack and the adaptations we make to survive in challenging environments will need to be unique to the individual, their circumstance and their version of depression or low mood. Treatment can vary, which is why we should be accepting of any method that someone finds helpful. From anti-depressants to hypnosis to cold water swimming, shamanic healers, mindfulness, Tibetan chanting, and running ultra-marathons – if it works for you, that is all that matters.

The second consequence of depression's rather impressive array of traits is how people might invalidate depression as a concept, their own depression, or someone else's depression. 'Zac, round the corner, says he's depressed but when my mate Sabina was depressed, she couldn't even go to work, but Zac is still as busy with work as ever.' Humans like to categorize and put things into boxes, but depression is more like a jumbled-up yard sale (one where someone forgot to put price tags on anything) so it can be hard for it to make sense. This questioning of validity can create stigma, which many of us will have felt, sadly. Much is picked up from societal messages or how we've been talked to or treated in the past. Downplaying or denying our own depression is often due to internalized stigma, as we attack ourselves with the critical narratives we're surrounded by – in the media, government, at work, and, unfortunately, even among friends and family. There are countless unhelpful and untrue opinions floating about out there.

As hard as I know this is, we should try not to worry about whether society believes in our depression; we can't change that right now. This is easier said than done, I realize. We are all influenced by the systems we live in, and life would be much easier if there was more understanding. The extent of that impact will be dictated by our background, upbringing, and levels of social and economic privilege, among other factors. There is much work to be done in creating accepting and safe spaces for anyone with a mental health issue and we may not see the positive change we hope for any time soon. This can feel deeply disempowering, and can, in turn, further worsen our mental health – feeling unaccepted is bad for anyone. The only way I feel able to counter this is by affecting change in my own environment and the people I surround myself with, any way that I can. That's why I harp on about mental health as I do – socially, professionally, at my spinning classes and anywhere I feel comfortable to do so.

We don't all have to speak up – it really can feel very difficult – but, if it feels helpful, you could try explaining the concept of the many depression disguises to your most important people. Depression is a master of disguises and every form it takes is valid, including yours.

Knowing your own depression disguise

For all its infinite variety, mine and others' depression share a few common truths. This can help us as we look out for depression being on the prowl. My depression is the least inventive thing to exist, showing up in the same way, with the same ugly exterior, as always: a sludge monster, moving at a glacial pace, leaving a trail of slime, commonly found on the sofa, smelling kind of bad. Depression really hasn't bothered to evolve, so we can quickly become familiar with its tell-tale signs. That doesn't always make it easy to spot – that would be far too simple! Depression will do its utmost to convince us that it's not depression ('You're just actually really shit', it'll tell us) so we can still miss it, even when it's covered top-to-toe in sludge. We'll be exploring ways that we can catch it out, even so.

For now, try thinking of your depression's defining or common characteristics. Do you feel depleted of energy? Do you think you're rubbish at things you've always been good at? Do you feel quieter? Knowing what we're dealing with is crucial in catching it out, so let's get our depression 'WANTED' sign pinned up in the forefront of our mind. The more we analyse that horrid slime ball (nose peg, gloves and apron advised), the less likely it is that it'll slither past us when we're not looking. I know that can feel hard – most of us would like to never revisit how depression made us feel again – and we need to assess if we feel ready to do this kind of work. But, if you do, understanding your own depression can be half the battle.

Is it okay to tell people?

If there were a club for people who found it difficult to tell others about their depression, I would have been Chief President. While I may be able to talk about depression now, it's taken work, and I still shy away from telling certain people in particular contexts. That's when I'm feeling okay. When I'm languishing in depression's ditch, you will not find me uttering a single word about it. Not to anyone, whatever my relationship with them (and I really have tried to make myself).

So, I don't assume that everyone will breeze into telling others that they're struggling – talking about depression is hard, because of the stigma we've explored and what that (wrongly) says about us (weak, lesser than, broken, useless, etc.). No one is obliged to tell anyone anything about their mental health; you don't owe anyone that privilege. That said, there are so many benefits to being able to let the right people in and to discussing it to whatever degree feels comfortable. Sharing can help relieve the weighty burden and attached guilt, while also helping others help us, which could hoist us out of our depression hole sooner. As tough as it feels, it's worth trying to work up to it, if you can.

As ex-Chief President of the 'Depression? What Depression?' Club, I have been on quite the journey (believe me, I thought I'd be the last person to write a book on the topic) but it still often feels simpler and more comfortable to keep quiet. When it comes to sharing our mental health experiences, I always say, 'It is never easy, but it does get easier.' I think it will always feel complicated to some degree but the more we do it, the 'easier' it gets.

I'm lucky that I work in a progressive company that values diversity and inclusion and creates a feeling of belonging – and that extends to our mental health. Even so, when I decided to tell my manager I was struggling with my mental health – which was a feat in itself, as I've never felt confident enough to do that in previous jobs – I was terrified. My depression doing its 'hide and seek' thing, I believed I was the problem, so I just about managed to squeeze out, 'I'm struggling, but I'm working on it.' My manager was wonderful and supportive, but I still disliked her knowing. I would dread every check-in thereafter when she'd ask me, 'How are you feeling...in yourself?' with nothing but empathy in her voice. While it wasn't comfortable, it was the best decision I made. I was supported where I might not have been and I had adjustments made which made working easier (such as not having to attend in-person team meetings). It was okay – good, even – that I had shared this thing I was, unjustly, embarrassed by and ashamed of.

There was also the Christmas run I went on with my mum. I had planned to tell her, 'I'm not doing too well', at some point as we trotted along the leafy roads of my childhood. Except, every time I tried, a tennis-ball-sized lump lodged in my throat and I could not make myself speak. As we neared the end of our run, by which point my nerves were providing a near-on out-of-body experience, I found the quiet words, 'I'm struggling, Mum', and burst into tears. Mum gave me the warmest and tightest of hugs, thanked me for telling her, and told me that everything was going to be okay. I still really didn't like my family knowing. I didn't feel deserving of their care and saw myself as an attention-seeking burden. I didn't have to tell my mum, but doing so was part of assembling my 'support crew' and giving myself a better chance at tossing depression in the dumpster. She was also thankful to have the opportunity to support me. I was anxious about the unwanted load and worry I might be placing on my parents, but it was okay that I told Mum that day – in fact, it was the best thing for all of us.

I give you these examples because I want to be real about how it can feel to tell people you are depressed, were depressed, or might be getting depressed – I want you to know that I get it. I also know that I have never received a negative response when I've told people. This isn't everyone's experience – it depends on how supportive and understanding our friends, family, colleagues, bosses, and others are, which can come down to education and open-mindedness, among other things. Despite a positive experience of being more open, I don't always feel confident or positive about it. Mental health, and our relationship with it, is complex beyond words, and it's understandable that sharing may not feel comfortable in its entirety – perhaps some bits feel manageable, while others don't. We can choose to embrace whichever parts we want.

It's time for a dose of realism. We often won't feel able to tell others – perhaps we might receive unfavourable treatment, have opportunities taken away from us, or have someone make unhelpful judgements about our character. Despite how inclusive and supportive my current employer is, would I have told them I'd been depressed multiple times at interview? Absolutely not. This is my version of self-protection in a world where, sadly, our mental health experiences won't always be met with the understanding and acceptance they deserve. So, I can't stress enough that it is up to us to decide when sharing feels helpful.

* * *

It is okay to tell people about what you've been through – if you wish to. There is no moral value attached to your depression or any other mental health condition; it doesn't make you a lesser human being. You should feel safe to tell those people who make you feel safe to tell them. In fact, 'safety' is the operative word and you should feel a sense of safety with anyone you choose to let in. Whatever you decide, please know it is okay that you have been, or are, depressed. It is also okay (and can be helpful) to tell people, if it feels right. In Chapter 8 we'll look at how we can approach those tricky-feeling conversations.

Mental health holes

It's hard to start conversations about mental health, as we've begun to explore. I am still not able to talk about my mental health with complete carefree abandon, for many reasons. Will other people judge us? Will it make them feel awkward? Is the label 'depression' too much? Does 'low mood' accurately convey just how shit we really feel? Is what we're feeling deserving of a label at all? Once we've decided on how we'd like to start the conversation, it takes bravery and courage to take that leap of faith and put your trust in the person you're telling. The truth is that there is no one out there for whom this conversation won't resonate on some level (everyone has felt shit, to some degree) and won't fill them with relief that they, too, can be honest about life's ups and downs.

That's why I came up with my 'mental health holes'. Depression can feel dark, isolating and inescapable; exactly like being stuck in a hole (I must stress, this is conjecture, and I've never tried being trapped in an actual hole). Before I'd even visualized these mental health holes, I noticed that I'd been describing my tussles with depression as feeling as if I was 'in a pit' or 'down a right hole'. It felt like the closest descriptor for the sheer hopelessness I had felt and the vastness of the task that lay ahead of me, to pull myself out of the depths.

But what had led to my hole sketching frenzy? I was in my usual Christmas slump, as the lack of routine and the eerie quiet of London, my friends having returned to their hometowns, doesn't suit me. However, this time I was panicking; I'd not long finished my last meeting with depression (way more insufferable than the worst work meeting in the world), and I wasn't ready to fall down a depression hole again.

I took a moment and tried to find some perspective. 'Hold on, I'm not down a dried-up well again. I'm just in a puddle, and I've got the footwear to deal with this.' It served as a reminder that our mental health and mood exist on a spectrum of 'really great' to 'really shit', and fluctuations are normal. It helped me put on my metaphorical wellies and plan how I could splash through this puddle with confidence and not a soggy sock in sight.

I wanted a more permanent reminder, so I took out pen and paper and roughly sketched out the range of holes I'd been down over my then ten-year mental health journey. Taking them in, I realized I now had an easy and simple way to communicate where I was, or had been, on my own mental health

WHICH MENTAL HEALTH HOLE ARE YOU IN?
HOLE 00
PUDDLE
TOTALLY MANAGEABLE WITH THE RIGHT FOOTWEAR.
SANDY GOLF BUNKER
THAT SAND CAN BE SURPRISINGLY TRICKY TO NAVIGATE.
POTHOLE
MAY BE SHORT-LIVED BUT CAN BE SURPRISINGLY LETHAL.
RIP
SHALLOW GRAVE PLOT
LOW FOOT FALL - COULD BE A WHILE BEFORE YOU'RE FOUND.
DRIED-UP WELL
THIRSTY WORK. NO ONE WOULD KNOW THAT YOU'RE GONE.
DEATH PIT
IT'S GOING TO TAKE SOME COMING BACK FROM THAT.

spectrum – and with a buoyant lightness that countered depression's doom and gloom. And the best thing about it? I didn't even have to utter the word 'depression' to communicate how I felt (life-affirming news, as someone who has often struggled to identify with the label).

I sent the drawing to a few best friends. Responses came back: 'Love this! I'm dragging my feet through a sandy golf bunker right now' or, 'Omg, I've totally hit a vicious pothole and it's wiped me out.' My friends were using my new language to describe how they felt. As I sat there in shock, I realized that half the battle is in finding a way to easily communicate so we feel connected and understood. That doesn't require a diagnosis or a medical label. This de-medicalized, visual way of communicating our mental health made it less scary, less intimidating and a damn sight easier for people to share. We had a shared visual language that didn't need explaining, that transcended the need for labels or stigmatized language, and it spoke volumes.

I also discovered the great power in being able to identify 'which mental health hole we're in', or where I was on the mood spectrum. My Christmas slump freak-out was not uncommon, many of us will know the terror of believing we're plummeting into low mood's depths again, which can send us spiralling. If you can locate your mental health on that spectrum, perhaps you'll be able to reassure yourself that you're not headed towards the unattended grave plot that you were in last year after all. By identifying my Christmas 'hole' as a puddle, I was able to keep my worry contained and hold on until I felt brighter. It is this awareness of our reality – whether we find ourselves in better or worse shape than we hoped – that is likely to drive the first step in any positive, helpful action we need to take.

This is a great time to revisit the 'recovery squiggle', from Chapter 1. It is important to remember that our mood will fluctuate daily based on memories, events, thoughts, fears and various events going on around us. My festive dip didn't mean I was in a depression death pit again; it was simply one shit day or week, and a very normal part of our ever-undulating mental health. It makes sense that I am sensitive to these peaks and troughs, given my experiences, but a dip in mood does not mean, 'Here we go again; depression is riding in on its stinky horse and tooting its horrible horn', nor is it 'only downwards from here'. Sometimes we'll be able to ride out the lows, and they may even be useful opportunities to practise steadying our Good Ship Mental Health and finding calmer waters.

The holes on my mental health spectrum are the ones that spoke to me on that December day a few years ago. As we know, there is no 'one size fits all' for depression and you are at liberty to choose your own set of holes that best represent your reality – that's their beauty! I wish I'd had the idea to include an uncovered manhole. Fine one moment, the next thing you know, you'll be sullenly sploshing around in the sewers before you can say, 'Who's in charge of health and safety around here?!' Feel free to get creative with it.

Irreverent and slightly silly though these holes might initially seem, their simplicity provides a powerful visual tool to communicate, rally your support network and get yourself choosing a plan to start feeling better. I'd love it if you used the concept of mental health holes (whether you adopt mine or invent your own) to reflect on how you're feeling – and even use it as a tool to encourage openness and embrace a common understanding among friends and family. The first step is often about finding a link with others, and a shared language or analogy is a brilliant way to get there. Don't worry if there isn't anyone around you to walk this path with right now. We'll come on to how – using your rope, ice picks and harness – you can scale the rocks and start searching out others to continue the journey with.

Identifying my festive season dip as a puddle calmed me down and then reassured me that I had the tools in my mental health survival kit to use to whip myself right out of my lowered mood funk (because that's all it turned out to be). Once we've identified the hole we're languishing in, we can kick-start the plan that we need in that moment – an escape plan, if you will. Sometimes we'll find a rickety old ladder to carefully climb, and at other times, we'll be calling in the helicopter rescue team. It all depends on which kind of hole you find yourself in. None are insurmountable and it's time to learn about kick-starting that plan.

• CHAPTER 4 •

Being Prepared to Kick into Action

The Plan Ecosystem

Before we get into the nitty gritty of plan making, we need to address what 'The Plan' is and the potential it holds.

The Plan is our approach to extricating ourselves from depression's swampy depths, by allowing us to plan and commit to a way forward. It will involve activity scheduling, it will hopefully involve your support crew, and you may well revisit it, revising parts where needed. The Plan is structured, quantifiable (where possible) and phased, based on our progress along our road to recovery. Once we have the basics right, it is a simple tool, but one that takes some careful consideration at the outset – and persistence, patience and self-compassion in the execution. If pitched right, it should push us just outside our Depression Comfort Zone (the limits depression likes to place on our life, to keep things how it likes), but not so much that it feels like an insurmountable challenge that we can't tackle. A little bit of discomfort is perfect; that's depression feeling all angsty that you're not giving in to it.

The Plan has always been what has saved me, in some capacity. I won't pretend that I have always made one at the first opportunity, or even stuck to the one I made with my therapist (avoidance is one of my depression superpowers). Sometimes, executing any plan feels downright impossible. Early in your recovery journey, you may feel too low or not have the energy to be proactive, which I can empathize with. Therefore, it's not without its challenges, but I know how helpful it can be to have in your depression toolbox.

The Plan does not exist in isolation (after all, 'no man [nor any plan] is an island'). It lives within an ecosystem: The Plan Ecosystem. As great as The Plan

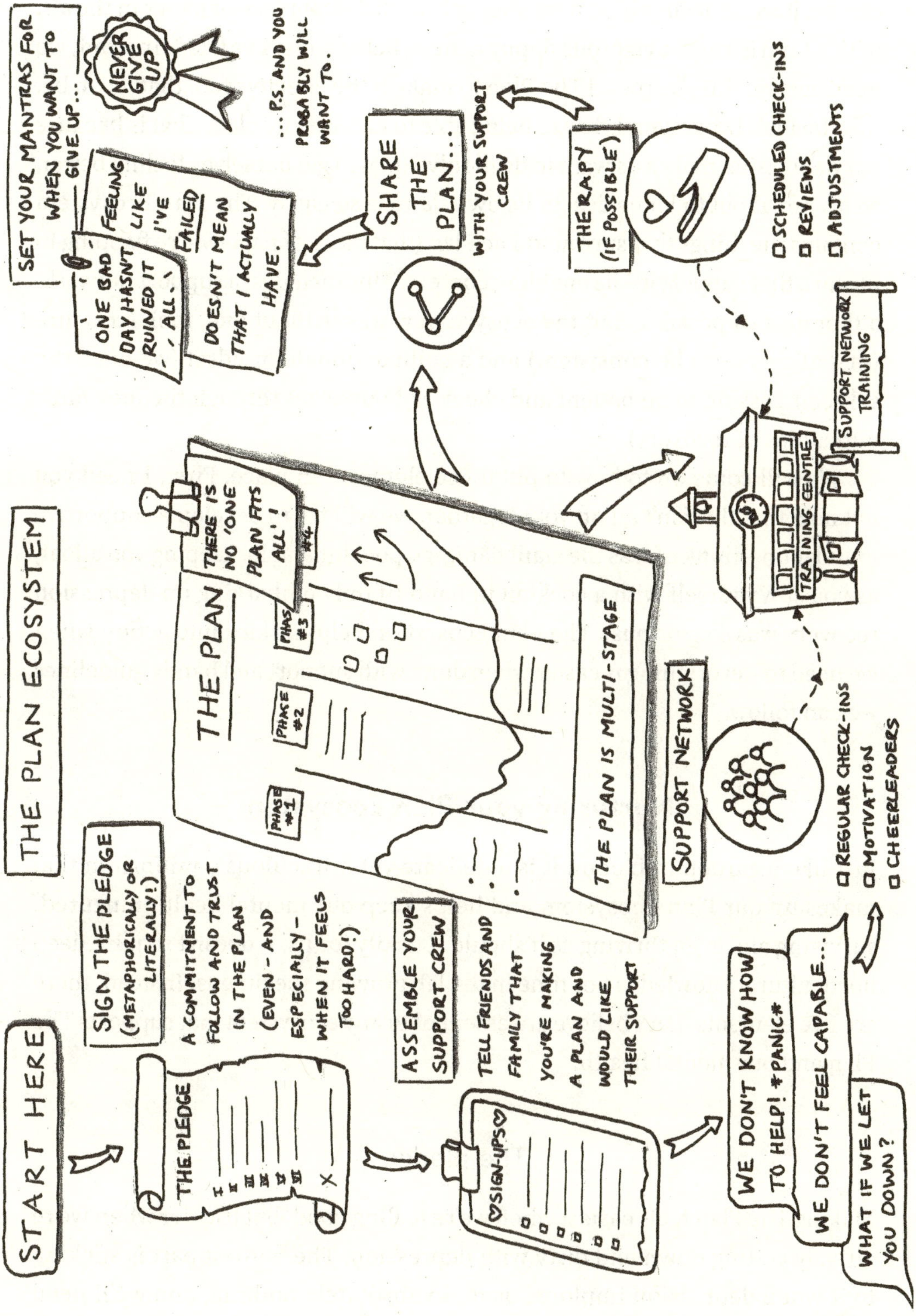
START HERE
THE PLAN ECOSYSTEM
THE PLEDGE
I II III IV V VI X
SIGN THE PLEDGE (METAPHORICALLY OR LITERALLY!)
A COMMITMENT TO FOLLOW AND TRUST IN THE PLAN (EVEN - AND ESPECIALLY - WHEN IT FEELS TOO HARD!)
SIGN-UPS
ASSEMBLE YOUR SUPPORT CREW
TELL FRIENDS AND FAMILY THAT YOU'RE MAKING A PLAN AND WOULD LIKE THEIR SUPPORT
WE DON'T KNOW HOW TO HELP! *PANIC*
WE DON'T FEEL CAPABLE...
WHAT IF WE LET YOU DOWN?
THE PLAN
PHASE #1
PHASE #2
PHAS #3
#4
THERE IS NO 'ONE PLAN FITS ALL'!
THE PLAN IS MULTI-STAGE
SUPPORT NETWORK
REGULAR CHECK-INS
MOTIVATION
CHEERLEADERS
TRAINING CENTRE
SUPPORT NETWORK TRAINING
SCHEDULED CHECK-INS
REVIEWS
ADJUSTMENTS
THERAPY (IF POSSIBLE)
SHARE THE PLAN...
WITH YOUR SUPPORT CREW
SET YOUR MANTRAS FOR WHEN YOU WANT TO GIVE UP...
NEVER GIVE UP
ONE BAD DAY HASN'T RUINED IT ALL.
FEELING LIKE I'VE FAILED DOESN'T MEAN THAT I ACTUALLY HAVE.
... P.S. AND YOU PROBABLY WILL WANT TO.

can be, it won't do anything if we simply brandish that piece of paper in the air, with a flourish and a vigorous flappy action. Believe me, I've tried. Instead, we need certain things around The Plan to make it the effective tool that it can be.

The Plan Ecosystem is key to being able to kick off any plan. That is because our depression makes us want to do diddly-squat to get ourselves feeling better, so it's not about to let us design its own demise so easily. The Plan Ecosystem contains the things that surround The Plan (that piece of paper we're flapping in the air), that support it – its enabling context. This includes: a support network, a therapist (if possible, but the ecosystem works without one, too), structure (that allows us to be consistent) and a compassionate mindset (we need the self-compassion to be patient and cheerlead ourselves through the inevitable difficulties of recovery).

We will come on to how to put those elements in place. First, I need you to know that this isn't all on you: together, we will try to develop a supportive foundation – think of it as the giant flamingo pool inflatable, keeping you afloat, as you sun yourself with a cocktail in hand (if only embarking on depression recovery was so glorious). The Plan Ecosystem helps us kick into action when we need to – everything is easier when done with support and handy guidelines we can follow.

Nurturing your Plan Ecosystem

Just like a garden in bloom, it is a delicate yet miraculous equilibrium that makes up our Plan Ecosystem and helps keep our mental health nurtured, surviving and even thriving as it should. Luckily for us, it doesn't require deep horticultural knowledge nor time in the lab growing specimens. Instead, there are five elements that I believe are essential to any ecosystem that supports The Plan and our mental health.

The pledge

Making The Plan feels easiest when we're feeling good, but trickier when we're already getting down and dirty with depression. The hardest part is sticking to it when depression implores us to do absolutely nothing, and we'll need something to keep us committed. Enter the pledge. We are swearing our solemn allegiance to our Plan, vowing that we will do what we can to invest in its execution. Without the pledge, it may feel all too easy to give up when difficulties arise (and they will, for all of us, because that's life).

You can write yours out and sign it with a flourish, if you like, but telling one of your support network is equally as good. The important thing is that we are committed to The Plan, even – and especially! – when it feels hard. There have been times when I was so terrified of planning any activity that my sister almost had to drag me, kicking and screaming, to put together my weekly activity schedule (which we'll explore soon). There may be times like that. But, rather annoyingly, beating depression is about doing a whole load of stuff we don't want to do. I'd recommend co-creating your pledge (and, for that matter, your Plan) with a trusted member of your support network and letting them hold you accountable throughout.

So, do you so solemnly declare your commitment to The Plan and all that it entails? If so, you are ready to sign the pledge.

The therapist

Whether the idea of therapy terrifies you, or has you investing all your hopes, dreams and aspirations in finding the right therapist for you, there is no doubt that therapy is usually helpful, and will be the cornerstone of many people's recovery plan, if they are able to access it. It is also often an ongoing tool used for people's mental health maintenance, wherever they are on the mental health spectrum. Therefore, it may be no surprise to see it in our Plan Ecosystem.

In Chapter 9, we'll explore whether therapy is right for you, and other avenues for support (including this book). A good therapist can help prop up your Plan Ecosystem and add an extra level of robustness to your safety net. Their experience and expertise can be invaluable. My first therapist had been a psychologist for 20 years – and had worked through depression with her clients countless times – when I turned up in her therapy room, feeling as if depression had dragged me through the low mood hedge backwards. None of us knows a sure-fire way out of depression, but an experienced therapist will know a number of tricks we can pull to leave depression dazed, confused and wondering whether to call it a day.

Without my first therapist, I wouldn't have had any idea where to start in making my plan. In fact, I wouldn't have even known that I could benefit from one. We made a good few plans over the years, tweaking and adapting where necessary, working out how to make them effective and suited to me, and in time, I learnt how to make them myself. My therapist would simply be there to challenge me or push me on parts that needed to take me a little more outside my Depression Comfort Zone. She was also there with a compassionate voice when I felt I was failing, or to give me permission to take my foot off the gas a little when I wasn't quite ready for such a leap.

Therapy is useful to so many people for so many reasons, and a therapist's role in enabling The Plan can be a mighty important one (and if they are trained in cognitive behavioural therapy, they'll be a dab hand at helping you with The Plan). If therapy isn't an option for you, fear not! There are other support avenues, and we can get your support network trained up and experts in The Plan (more on this in Chapter 8).

The support crew

I would be nowhere without the wonderful, patient, kind souls that make up my support network or, as I like to call them, my 'support crew'. They are the friends and family who have stuck by my side when the going has got tough, in the days when depression was new to me and to us, to now, when we understand my mental health better than we used to. They've shown understanding and willingness to learn, given me space when needed, and turned up at my door when space was what I craved but wasn't what I needed for my recovery.

We'll learn more about our support crew in Chapter 8, including how to build and lean on yours. For now, know that those people in your life whose love, care and support you can rely on are qualified to help you with your Plan. If our Plan Ecosystem is a garden with a wonderful but delicate equilibrium, think of our support network as the water that keeps it alive and thriving. With a little training in The Plan, your support crew are more than qualified to understand the importance of this tool and to guide you through making one together.

A structure

One of my defining memories of my seven run-ins with depression involved feeling utterly directionless. I felt stuck while also perplexingly lost, as though I was floating through space, untethered, yet not looking for a place to tie myself to. My lack of a plan, but also a lack of structure, was a huge contributor to that feeling.

Structure in The Plan Ecosystem is crucial to allow us to execute a reliable plan. It will help us feel that we have more control over a life which has recently felt as if anybody but ourselves is directing it. So, when my therapist and I first put a plan together, that 'floating' feeling – which, ultimately, underpinned much of my hopelessness – began to disappear. I had a goal, I had a means of achieving it, and we'd be using planning, structured activities and incremental steps to get there. This gave me hope that I was consciously working towards a life that felt better, which felt empowering (a tall feat when consumed by depression's hopelessness).

Structure – that can be daily or weekly routines, plans and schedules, regular check-ins and more – makes it easier to stick to our pledge. We can say that we're committed to The Plan, but unless we put in place tools to facilitate that, even our very best intentions may be little more than intentions. Of course, factor in room for flexibility and a break on the odd day when a plan simply feels too much. It's all part of creating sustainable routines, habits and regular practices, to keep us accountable through action, which will hopefully lead to incremental growth. Progress yields more progress, and small steps every day can have a wonderful snowball effect for our self-worth, self-esteem and confidence.

Your self-compassion

Prized the world over, but rarely found in abundance, self-compassion can do wonders for us. It instructs us to go easy on ourselves when that toxic, scathing, critical inner voice is telling us that we're shit at everything. It reminds us of our worth and that no one is perfect. It gives us perspective and helps us acknowledge that we're all simply making it up as we go along and doing our best. We, and our Plan, are in much safer hands when cradled in the gentle yet supportive hold of self-compassion.

There are times on this journey that we will absolutely feel like a failure. Nothing will feel as if it's going right, and progress may feel non-existent or too microscopic to notice – and, to top it all, we'll still be feeling shit. In those moments, self-compassion will tell us not to quit. It pipes up with its voice of kindness to remind us, 'You're doing your best and that is more than good enough' or, 'Okay, things aren't going to plan today; not every day will, but tomorrow is a fresh start.' Depression thrives off negativity so it actively fans the flames of our harsh inner critic. Self-compassionate affirmations can extinguish depression's toxic flames of negativity, restoring reason and perspective. We can be so kind to ourselves that depression decides to skedaddle and find something else to set on fire (preferably a dustbin its climbed into). We may feel powerless, but, in actual fact, we're the very best person to send it scuttling.

One of the recent ideas I've explored with my current therapist is that how we talk to ourselves when our mental health is good may impact how we talk to ourselves when we're doing our best hole-dwelling act, and our mental health is less good. Wheeling out the self-compassion on demand when our mood is in the gutter feels absurd – I get it. Most of us find it hard to treat ourselves with kindness even when we're feeling tip-top. However, the chances of finding a dose of self-compassion when depression's back is turned and its voice is fainter are much higher if we're used to speaking to ourselves in a compassionate and loving way when things feel brighter. This may not be easy – my inner critic has been part of the furniture for decades, using it to motivate myself to do better – but it is possible. In Chapter 12, we'll explore ways to nurture our internal compassion. We want to be able to say, 'Ah, my old friend self-compassion – here just when I need you', when depression turns up, rather than, 'Sorry, self-what?'

* * *

While I have shared a few top tips to get you started, the reality is that our Plan Ecosystem is stitched into the very fabric of our life – the preparations, adjustments and safety nets that enable us to come to our own rescue, with the support of others, when times get tough. None of us want a ticket to Depression's Comeback Tour – memories of the first concert are too unforgettable, and not in the good way, so most of us will do what we can to 'depression-proof' our life.

That's The Plan Ecosystem, and you probably care for yours in some capacity already, without necessarily realizing it. Put simply, it's 'looking after ourselves', on the good and bad days, however our mental health is. This is my reminder to spend a little time nurturing yours. Nothing would bring me more joy than to see all of us, together, proactively keeping our Plan Ecosystems alive and thriving.

* CHAPTER 5 *

Making a Plan to Help Yourself

Getting started with The Plan: The timetable

The science of psychology tells us that activity scheduling is good for us and our depression. By 'activity scheduling' I mean making a daily or weekly plan, which lays out the various activities that you commit to doing each day. It could be a mixture of hobbies and pleasurable activities, as well as chores and must-dos, like doing the laundry or making the beds (all have their place in recovery).

How I explain the usefulness of activity scheduling, as someone who is definitely not a scientist, is that depression thrives on emptiness. It's akin to giving it a deserted playground and saying, 'Off you go – play!' Soon, it's graffitied the walls, ripped the nets from the basketball hoops, knocked over all the bikes and upended the rubbish bins. You've got a depression-unruly situation on your hands, and it feels impossible to sort out.

Depression creates, but also thrives on, the inactivity that a relatively empty life brings. It allows its negative voice to be heard at full volume and ensures that we have no counter evidence to remind our brain of things we used to enjoy, the joy we can feel and the vibrant person we truly are. The logical counter to this is to gradually fill that emptiness. It may take some time to build up to, especially if we've spent a long time doing very little; doing more will probably feel overwhelming initially. But we can take it at our own pace – I've gone from months of nothing to trying just one activity a day for weeks, and that was as admirable a starting point as any.

Doing the doing (even when it seems pointless)

Depression will tell us that all this will achieve nothing. I found trying to 'do more' terrifying and pointless – the thought of going out and doing things made my skin crawl, and I simply didn't believe it would work. Try convincing yourself to do a scary thing that feels like a total waste of time – it's far from easy! Don't be put off if this feels hard. We can think of this as a 'trial' of sorts. We're testing the theory that increasing activity will have a positive impact on mood, and then using the information we gather through the 'doing' to develop our Plan.

When we think about activity scheduling (or, as I like to call it, scheduling the shit out of depression) the trick is to split each day into regular 'chunks', with manageable activities and targets. This will get us used to a daily and weekly rhythm, as well as reminding us what it's like to have something to do throughout the day. It's important to plan and review each 'chunk' independently – as its own separate entity – so that if we don't meet our target or complete an activity (and, trust me, this will happen a lot, for all of us), it doesn't colour how we perceive the next 'chunk' and how capable we feel to take on the next activity.

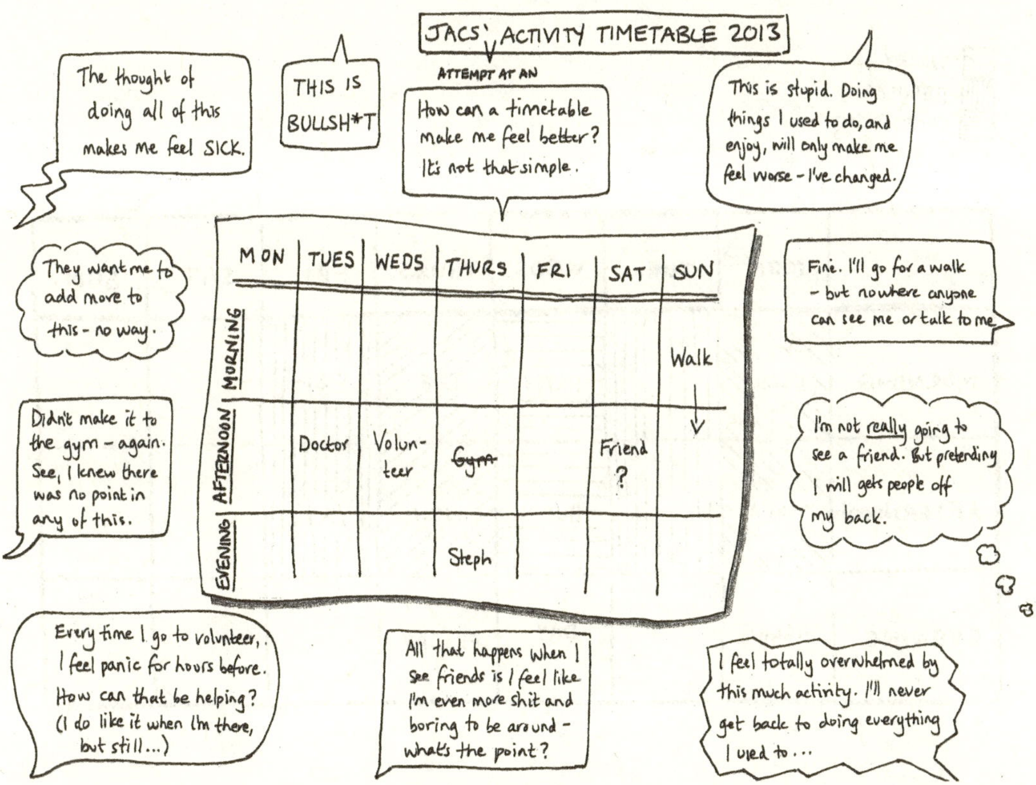

You can chunk your day into three sections – morning, afternoon and evening, as in the following tables. This works particularly well if you aren't working and don't have much structure in your day, but you are welcome to split up your day to fit around work or other regular commitments (I've shared a second table, which can be adapted to fit your schedule).

	MON	TUES	WEDS	THURS	FRI	SAT	SUN
MORNING							
AFTERNOON							
EVENING							

WORK/ REGULAR COMMITMENTS

	MON	TUES	WEDS	THURS	FRI	SAT	SUN
MORNING	URGH		HAPPY	THE	FRI-		
AFTERNOON	MONDAY		HUMP	NEW	YAY!		
EVENING	AGAIN?!		DAY	FRIDAY			

Now here comes a hard truth: you won't want to do most, or any, of this – but you will need to try and make yourself do it as best you can. Pretend I've shouted that through a megaphone to drown out depression, which will take this opportunity to pipe up even louder, reminding you once more that this is all a waste of time and will only make you feel worse. Thankfully, we're getting better at identifying depression's ranty voice so we can learn to ignore it, take the leap and go for it – as hard as it feels. We can build up to our end goal but trying to tackle even one or two activities or tasks to start with will have you on the right track.

This is when having a support crew by our side is invaluable, for that gentle encouragement (or a sterner word or two if you're receptive to a bit of 'tough love', as I am) and a reminder that we really can achieve more than we ever thought possible. Tell them about your weekly activity schedule and let them in on The Plan.

Mastery and pleasure

When my therapist introduced me to the concepts of 'mastery' and 'pleasure' it blew my mind. There are activities possessing these seemingly magical qualities that, if combined in beautiful symbiosis, can be used to build an upward spiral of mood and energy.

It turns out there's no magic here. Simply put, different activities we do have different roles. There are those activities which enhance a feeling of achievement (mastery) and those which are (or, if depressed, have previously been) enjoyable (pleasure). If you think about finishing that jumper you've been knitting for three months (mastery) versus eating a delicious meal (pleasure), we can start to understand the different satisfaction each activity brings. Our job is to schedule a range and balance of such activities which are likely to be meaningful, and provide a sense of mastery and pleasure, to best boost our mood. Across a week, we should aim to have a good mix of the two.

When depression is telling you that everything is abhorrent and pointless, and nothing in this world will ever bring you joy again, it's going to feel hard to think of things that will feel remotely enjoyable or satisfying. Your support crew will be full of ideas for you – you could try brainstorming together! Doing supposedly enjoyable activities may not bring you any pleasure initially, but this relies on trusting the process – you will get there in the end. A good start is to focus on small outstanding tasks (e.g. doing the washing up, tidying that messy junk drawer, or moving the clothes from your 'floordrobe' into the wardrobe). These tasks can be a great way of building your sense of achievement. You never know, seeing the job finally done might just give you a sense of pleasure you hadn't expected.

Avoiding avoidance

Depression has even the least avoidant of us carting out every excuse under the sun to try and get out of going through with The Plan – there won't be an excuse out there that we don't try to use.

So, if you'll allow me, I'd like us to get a whole bunch of them out of the way right now:

* I'm too tired.
* It's been a difficult week.
* Work is tough/I'm out of work at the moment.
* My mum/dad/sister/partner is unwell.
* I'll do it when I feel fitter/have a job/feel better.
* I look too awful.
* Today doesn't feel like 'my day'.
* It's a day of the week ending in 'y'.

We will find these, and many more, excuses to not get started. However, I need to be very clear: the timing will never feel right. That is because we're engaging with The Plan, and scheduling activities, at a time when we don't feel ready to. It all feels like a huge stretch, and we've spent a long time practising being very 'unstretched'. However, if we don't start, recovery will never be ours, and, believe me, when you're out the other side, it feels like the best hug you've ever received in your life. I gently ask that you suspend your disbelief, tuck your ambivalence away in a box, leave any scepticism at the door and give this crazy notion that recovery, or feeling better than you do, is possible from today, and give it a good go.

Introducing The Plan Pie

Every plan is unique to the individual, a combination of what works for them (things they like or used to like doing, before depression took over) and how far into their depression pit they are. It's time to explore how we make The Plan, and it's going to take a bit of baking: our very own delicious plan Pie – the tastiest thing about low mood! The Plan Pie (see the next page) is a way of visualizing the various elements that go in The Plan, all of which contribute positively to improving your mood and quality of life.

If you don't have much faith in a plan, I understand – nor did I. While our hearts tell us that all we wish for is a way out of depression, our heads will find it hard to believe that there's anything out there that can help – not least something as basic and unsexy as 'a plan'. That's because experience tells us that depression feels totally unfathomable and almost completely insurmountable. What's more, sometimes it's hard to see the link between the effort we put in and the incremental improvements we'll make, if we even notice them at all – I always said my recovery 'just sort of happened'. Whether we know it or not, it's because we've been tucking into a delicious Plan Pie.

But now I have developed a deep love for The Plan. I hold a deep admiration for its versatility too as there really is no 'one plan fits all'. Yours might be an 'I'm just in a little depression puddle' plan, or perhaps 'I'm down a dried-up depression well, I've felt so low, for so long, I can't remember another way to be' plan. Every circumstance is different, albeit linked by a common thread: we need a route out of our depression hole and a process to get there.

I'm hoping that if I can be a convert to The Plan, you'll give it a try with me.

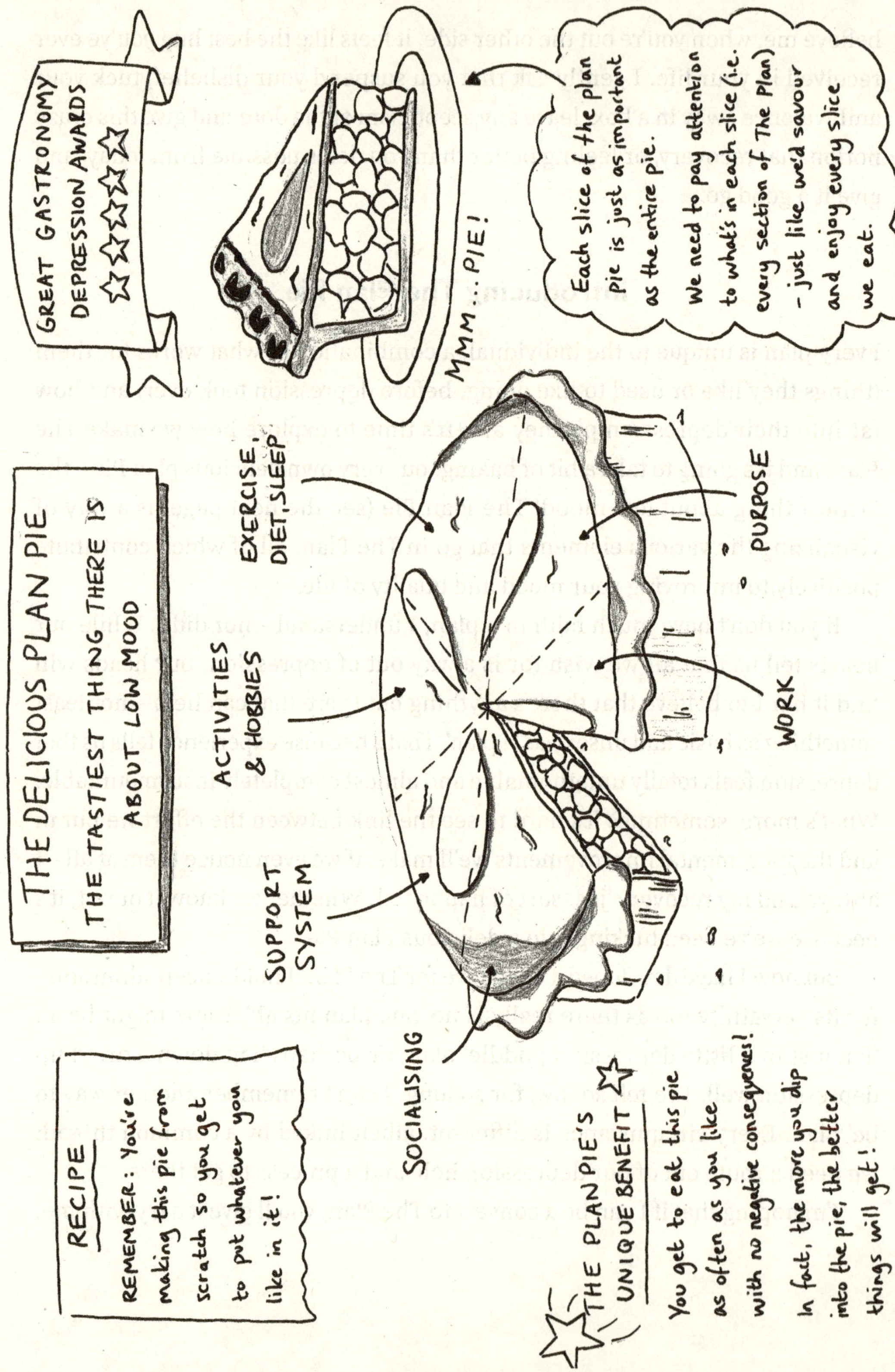
THE DELICIOUS PLAN PIE
THE TASTIEST THING THERE IS ABOUT LOW MOOD
GREAT GASTRONOMY DEPRESSION AWARDS
MMM...PIE!
Each slice of the plan pie is just as important as the entire pie.
We need to pay attention to what's in each slice (i.e. every section of The Plan) – just like we'd savour and enjoy every slice we eat.
EXERCISE, DIET, SLEEP
PURPOSE
ACTIVITIES & HOBBIES
WORK
SUPPORT SYSTEM
SOCIALISING
RECIPE
REMEMBER: You're making this pie from scratch so you get to put whatever you like in it!
THE PLAN PIE'S UNIQUE BENEFIT
You get to eat this pie as often as you like with no negative consequences!
In fact, the more you dip into the pie, the better things will get!

What should go into your Plan?

A focus on 'mastery-' and 'pleasure'-based activities, which we explored earlier in the chapter, gives us a great starting point and a few golden rules when choosing how to fill our Plan Pie. It can give us confidence that we're prioritizing helpful activities that can maximize our chances of feeling better.

Looking at our Plan Pie, I've pulled out some activity categories – or pie slices – that I believe help anyone lead a life that feels good: socializing and connection; a support system; activities and hobbies; exercise, diet and sleep; purpose; and work. That doesn't mean that we'll always feel incredible or that we'll feel satisfied with the filling in every pie slice at any given time. There will be ups and downs, downright shitty circumstances and times where we can't focus on what we need to – that's life for you.

The relative importance of each pie slice is unique to you. In my case, if I don't get so much as a whiff of an exercise-induced endorphin every day, you'll find me slinking towards the low mood gutter. Meanwhile, perhaps you prefer the calm satisfaction of baking a great cake (my first therapist's favourite well-being activity, which happens to combine mastery and pleasure!). Your delicious Plan Pie need only be the tastiest (and most helpful) morsel going for you alone.

If you can, I recommend calling on your trusted support crew as early as you can in the process. Think of them as sous chefs in your pie-making kitchen, helping you craft that delicious pastry. We know that support is instrumental in kicking depression to the curb, so why not roll your collective sleeves up and get making The Plan together. You may like a therapist to help (therapists with experience in cognitive behavioural therapy will be familiar with much of this approach) but you don't need one. Support can come from a sibling, partner, friend or parent – anyone who can help you think of a balanced collection of activities and habits (especially when our Depression Voice is getting in the way).

Now it's time to sit down and write or draw out your Plan, inserting activities and habits that fit your pie slice categories and that you used to enjoy and feel fulfilled by. All categories are helpful, but my advice is that *feeling connected and socializing*, a *support system* and a sense of *purpose* should feature in everyone's Plan Pie – they've proven transformative for everyone I speak to. You can then use the list of activities you come up with to populate the timetables that I shared earlier in the chapter (doing your best to have each pie slice represented in your week's schedule). Maybe you'll want to vary the size of each slice over time and as your mood changes (e.g. you may find socializing too overwhelming to do much of at first, so you might allocate that a small slice that gradually grows).

Thinking of things to do with your time can be hard when depression is telling you that everything is miserable. So, here are a few ideas to get you started.

Feeling connected and socializing	Support system	Exercise, diet, sleep
Do you find it easier to socialize one-to-one or in a group situation when feeling low? Whichever feels best, start with that. Some suggestions are more light touch, some are a more regular commitment. Assess what feels right, while remembering to test the boundaries of your comfort zone when you can. • Search online for local groups to connect with like-minded people (e.g. shared interests) or people in a similar situation (mental health support and peer groups). • Search your WhatsApp or DMs – is there anyone who has been trying to catch up with you but that you have ignored until now? Perhaps send a text and arrange a walk? • Meet for a coffee (somewhere quiet if that feels more manageable). • Go to the cinema (but meet for a chat and to choose your pick 'n' mix together first to up the social element). • Meet a friend for a walk. • Go to the shops and chat with the cashier. • Have a chat with your hairdresser. • If you have children, try chatting to other mums at nursery or school drop-off. Or try joining your school's parent teacher association. • Volunteer in a charity shop (there's likely to be a range of opportunities).	These aren't activities so much as doing what you can to enlist support, build a social circle, and check-in with those who support you. • Start perusing local community and activity group listings online and in local papers, to make new connections. • Consider a weekly check-in with friends and family. • Practise going to your support network when you are really struggling, as they can help you get back on track. • Consider working with a therapist (if possible – I understand that it's often not an accessible option, sadly).	The key here is to make it sustainable and enjoyable. I believe that there's a pleasurable way to be active for everyone – experiment until you find yours. It's hard to find the energy to cook when feeling low, but we can look forward to nutritious and tasty meals by keeping it simple. And a bedtime routine will make it easier to develop good sleeping habits. • Schedule exercise sessions for the week. If you're doing none or are new to it, start with one or two – write them on your timetable for accountability. • Try exercising or being active with a friend or family member – it takes the pressure off! • Eat three meals a day and avoid food that doesn't make you feel good, like junk food (especially before bed). • Keep a regular sleep routine. Try and go to bed at the same time every night and aim to sleep for six to nine hours. If you've been over-sleeping, it's time to make your alarm your best friend. • Avoid phones and devices for at least an hour before bed.

<table>
<tr><th>Activities and hobbies</th><th>Work</th><th>Purpose</th></tr>
<tr>
<td>This is the 'what did you used to enjoy?' section. If you can't remember or don't think you'll enjoy it anymore, give something new a go – perhaps with a friend if you're nervous. With all of these, the more social you can make them (e.g. joining a group, getting friends together) the better.
• Painting/drawing.
• Writing (fiction, non-fiction, poetry, journalling, random thoughts – anything!).
• Going for walks with friends and family.
• Gardening.
• Knitting/ crocheting/embroidery (use YouTube tutorials if you're a total newbie).
• Pottery/woodwork.
• Cooking/baking (this is really enjoyable to do for loved ones).
• Singing/acting/amateur dramatics/improv.
...anything that takes your fancy!</td>
<td>There is no requirement to work when depressed but, if you're able to, it can be great for your mental health as it keeps you busy and gives you tasks to focus on and a sense of purpose.
If you find yourself out of work but think a job is manageable, consider trying a part-time job, ideally where you can be part of a team and that is low stress. Volunteering – which can also be part-time – can be just as effective in a less pressured way.
If you feel work would add unneeded pressure, there are other valuable ways to gain a sense of purpose.</td>
<td>Every human wants to feel that they have a reason to be here, a 'purpose'. Depression often tells us we're a waste of space, so it's more important than ever to foster that sense of purpose.
• Volunteering – the perfect combination of purpose, structure and socializing. Volunteering has saved me more than I can explain. There are a whole range of opportunities – try an animal shelter, a charity shop, an environmental project, a youth group or hospital befriending, for example. Start with a weekly shift and see how you go. The cause is less important than the 'doing' at this stage (though it's great to choose one you care about).</td>
</tr>
</table>

* * *

While I used to be cynical, The Plan now feels deeply reassuring. This isn't the case when I'm feeling low (far from it!) but, like many things in life, we try to do it because it's good for us. Even so, we know that when struggling, things we plan that are 'good for us' will seem too overwhelming, and they probably won't feel nice (because we're pushing depression out of its comfort zone and it's kicking up a fuss like a big baby). But persevere – you will eventually start to feel differently about it all.

* CHAPTER 6 *

Making The Plan Sustainable

Pitching The Plan

Peeling ourselves away from depression is much about timing and pacing. Push ourselves too far, too soon, and we're likely to put ourselves off entirely, because it'll feel too difficult. Equally, if we allow ourselves to feel too settled and comfortable for too long, we're unlikely to see the change we hoped for. The gradient of change is never easy to assess, especially as everything that is good for us is likely to feel 'bad' and counter-intuitive at first. A good measure, or aim, is for each week, fortnight, month (or whatever pace of change feels manageable) to feel as if it's building on, and making progress from, the period before. Activity can be upped in intensity or quantity; for example, going on a group outing with friends, if you've felt more comfortable seeing just one friend, or scheduling more social opportunities.

Rome wasn't built in a day, and nor is our glowing mental health! We should aim for a reasonable pace that suits us, and we can gauge this as we go. It's important that we're outside our Depression Comfort Zone just enough that the progress we see motivates us to do more, but not so much that we overwhelm ourselves into running back to our depression dungeon. I want you to hold this idea of 'pacing' in mind – both when you feel as if you should be further along, sooner, and when you're perhaps feeling a little too comfortable to see any change.

Of course, none of our journeys will be identical nor navigated in the same way. It will depend on how long you've been down that depression hole and how deep it is. For those who have their support crew hammering at their door at the first sign of their quieter, more withdrawn self, you might feel more encouraged to resume the social activities you used to enjoy (even if they feel temporarily awkward and uncomfortable). It may be easier to pick up threads of your 'old' life, like going along to your mates' weekly pub get-together, turning up to book club, even if it's been months since you last went, or saying 'yes' to that run with your running buddy that you'd been dreading.

However, if your depression hole is looking more Grand Canyon than 'sandy golf bunker', or if you don't have an obvious support crew yet, it will take a bit more planning and perseverance. You'll need to be proactive in creating opportunities to make your life feel full again – always starting at a point that is just about manageable and building from there. Try reminding yourself of what you *used* to enjoy, if you can't think of anything you currently do. There is a vast array of meetup options, available through platforms like Meetup and Eventbrite, and specialized communities, such as OutSavvy for queer events, in the UK. Or, try checking your local newspaper or picking up flyers at your nearest library for shared interest groups. I've included more online meetup sources on my website (details are at the back of the book).

Pitching The Plan right is such an important part of giving ourselves a fighting chance at getting to where we'd like to be. Checking-in with a therapist can be immensely helpful, but checking-in with yourself can be equally useful. You know how you feel along this journey of 'trying to do more'. It's going to take a good dose of honesty, however – especially, if we've been taking things a little too easy and chilling out in our Depression Comfort Zone. Most importantly, please do this at your own pace (I don't care that Bob did it in two months – well done, Bob, but it's not a competition). Take stock of your achievements and your progress and use that to propel yourself forward. It might start off as a slow crawl (that's how most of us start, including myself), but one day I hope you'll feel closer to flying.

Are you evaluating your Plan fairly?

I'm no clairvoyant, but when you start to review your recovery journey progress, I can predict that your self-evaluation will sit somewhere between 'utterly shit' and 'not good enough'. We're still wearing our low mood specs, so everything is viewed through that grimy lens of 'I'm terrible, useless and a failure.' We need to find a system that allows us to evaluate our progress without this distorted view.

My first therapist would use a courtroom analogy to illustrate this. Imagine you're in court on a false allegation. It's no good only being presented with incriminating evidence from the prosecution without the defence's counter-argument. It's our job, when assessing how we're doing, to make sure we get a fair and honest 'hearing', making room for the good *and* the not so good. That way, we know when to keep going with more of the same or when to push ourselves a little more.

Depression will do its best to prevent you from hearing any of the information that will assist in changing your mind about yourself. The 'prejudice model' helps us understand why this is. It starts with our 'core beliefs' – or deeply held beliefs – about ourselves, other people and the world. These are often formed in early life and reinforced by external events. For example, a child may come to believe that they're 'bad' if they are constantly criticized, and verbally abused, by their parents. This influences their behaviour at school, where they're frequently punished for misbehaving, further reinforcing the idea that they're 'bad'. This develops into a 'core belief', which persists into adulthood, and continues to colour their life experiences. When depression is hanging around, we're even more likely to reject any information that doesn't fit in with these centrally held core beliefs that help maintain a negative view of ourselves and our circumstances. Therefore, we're going to learn how to evaluate whether the things you assume are 'facts' are actually so, or whether they are based on a one-sided and skewed perspective (spoiler: they're often the latter).

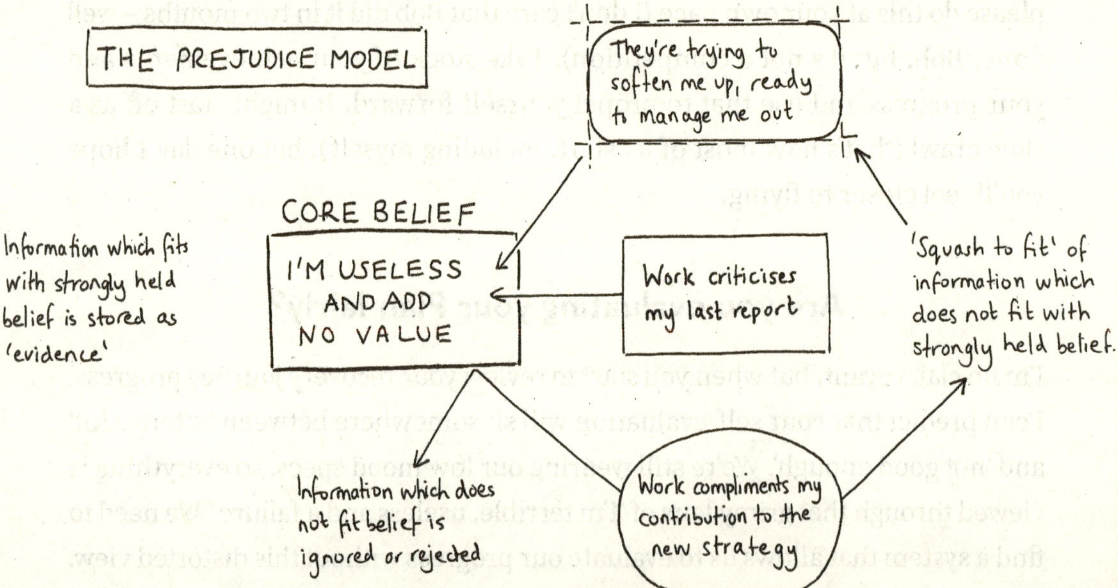

Think you've given up? Think again

On your quest to not give up on recovery, you are likely to 'give up' multiple times – or so it might seem (and that bit is important). I've got through seven recoveries, but I 'gave up' countless times along the way – or so I told myself. I often felt so hopeless and disempowered that continuing felt almost impossible. But I found a way to keep going; I hadn't really given up.

What did those times when I felt I'd given up (but hadn't) look like?

There was the time that, instead of going to my best friend's birthday party, I committed to working on my dent in the sofa, binge-watching *Selling Sunset*, and surviving on a diet of junk food and bitter disappointment in myself. By not going, I let the narrative of 'You're a useless person and a shit best friend. This is just who you are now' take over. I felt I might as well give up, so I told myself that I had.

Then there was the 2km run I dragged myself round, my leaden body screaming at me to stop. Instead of congratulating myself for the first run I'd done in months, I beat myself up, reminding myself that I used to float through 5km with ease. I vowed, 'That's the last run I'm going on, you piece of shit' and promptly gave up – or so I told myself.

Sometimes, it was thinking that I could never text back a friend because I hadn't replied for two months. 'That's it, the friendship is over and she hates me now', a narrative which amounted to giving up on our relationship and the potential to revive it.

These are just three examples of countless times I thought that I'd decided to give up. In that moment, I suppose I had. Depression is amazing at making us give in to unhelpful urges that exacerbate our low mood (but make life extra cozy for depression) – social isolation, minimal activity, not exercising self-compassion. It becomes a vicious circle – depression makes us feel ashamed to be who we are, we do less, we feel more ashamed that we're so useless, and so it continues. It's easy to see why we 'give up'.

But what if I told you that after I didn't turn up to that party, I decided to keep trying? A tiny part of me hoped that one day I might turn up to a social gathering – I wasn't resigned to never seeing my friends ever again, so I had to keep trying. Eventually I started meeting up with the odd friend, then a group, and today I enjoy a party as much as I ever did. I temporarily abandoned running, but I eventually opted for another form of exercise instead, to get my endorphins, which I know I prize. I also found it in me to send the best friend I'd been ignoring that text, after a year of no real contact. Of course, she didn't hate me, was so pleased to hear from me, and we met up, talked, cried, and we're still best friends now.

There is a supremely important distinction to note here: I didn't give up on any of these occasions – I simply believed that I had.

That is more than okay. As humans, in a moment of frustration we'll vow, 'I'm never doing that again!' We can be so invested in getting out of our depression hole that we're bound to feel upset, frustrated, exhausted, disappointed, and wish we were doing better – this is quintessentially human of us. But – and this is an enormous 'but' – we keep moving.

When thinking about 'not giving up' on recovery, or feeling better, it's most useful to think about our effort across the whole stretch of that journey. Our 'recovery squiggle' from Chapter 1 reminds us that progress will fluctuate, at times making us feel as if we're failing. This is all part of it, and we have the resilience to ride those moments out. Friends and family can be invaluable here. Why not try telling them how that missed run or cancelled-on social occasion made you feel. They really can be our biggest cheerleaders, reminding us that we're doing amazingly well, however we feel about our efforts. Getting back into exercise didn't just take the two weeks of hating myself for that horrible run. It took months of cajoling myself, experimenting and promising to myself that I'd stick with something eventually, even though I didn't believe it. As I pushed on, I questioned whether I was making any progress at all, and all the while depression goaded me and told me to give up (it really is a broken record). Getting over low mood is a whole lot of seeing perceived failure as a chance to get up and try again – and that's not easy, but the more we do it, the better we get at it.

Depression lies and it will do its utmost to convince you that you want to, or have, given up. In some moments, it will seemingly win, and you'll throw your hands up and proclaim, 'That's it – I'm done with this rubbish!' We're allowed to 'give up' temporarily – but it is only until we can regroup and go again. If you feel as if you've given up, there's every chance that this isn't the end.

What if you don't have a plan?

But what if you don't have a helpful plan, or any plan at all? Perhaps you haven't had the support you've needed to make and stick to one, or don't know where to start. Don't worry – I've found my way out of depression without a plan, and on my own, as I kept my depression to myself. While I wouldn't recommend it, I muddled my way through as best as I could, and I'm proud of those moments too.

If you're struggling with a plan, try starting just one regular activity you traditionally enjoyed; if you can fill a couple of different pie slice categories with it, all the better – it can lead to greater things. When I was 'plan-less', I knew I needed to do *something* to make a change. I apprehensively signed up to some volunteering shifts and nervously put a couple of group exercise classes in my diary, to combine exercise and connection. While they had been hard to commit to, I found a gentle enjoyment in the 'doing' (though disliked some bits), stuck with it, and that was the beginning of my climb out of my dried-up depression well.

Please don't worry if you haven't been able to make, or follow, a plan. The most important thing is that you try, when you can, to take elements of The Plan Pie and sprinkle them throughout your life – just a light dusting, or as much as you can, when you can. Maybe you have a Plan Pie but can only manage a little bite of it every now and again; socializing on the days you feel up to it, knitting at home rather than joining a club, and popping out for a short run on the days you're worshipping the TV binge-watching gods (I've put in my time with them too!).

If you're taking steps to reintroduce things you used to enjoy in your life, you should feel exceptionally proud of yourself.

* CHAPTER 7 *

Putting The Plan into Action

Donning the cape: Rescuing ourselves

Trying to get a one-way ticket out of depression can feel like constantly missing the bus when you're standing in the pouring rain. Imagine there was a bus that could whisk us away from it all (chance would be a fine thing), I'd be rocking up to that bus stop, an hour late, wondering why I was still stuck in the middle of nowhere. I'd have been totally oblivious that there was even a timetable. I always feel a little bit late noticing depression.

Unfortunately, nothing – not even a benevolent bus driver – is going to save us from our depression. That trying task is firmly down to us – and the earlier we get to it, the better. While our red, four-wheeled saviour might not exist, I believe we can be our own superhero, donning our cape and rescuing ourselves (with help, of course) from being down depression's dingy hole.

That might take the form of our pledge to The Plan (just like we talked about in our Plan Ecosystem in Chapter 4); it might be starting up a new gym habit; it might be being honest for the first time with parents or friends. 'Donning the cape' is a mindset that accepts and embraces the agency – and power – we have in determining our onward course. Don't worry, I can still feel powerless to the whims of my mental health when depression descends, so I'm not suggesting that you need to feel totally in control nor that it's all down to you. However, if we remember that tucked in our depression toolbox is our very own superhero cape, it might just help us to take back even the smallest bit of control and influence. That, to me, is life-changing.

I'll say it again: none of this is easy. Despite my bus-missing frustrations, I know I should show myself compassion because depression can be inordinately hard to sniff out, and then stand up to when it's bullying us around. In fact, most of us aren't sure how to 'don the cape', or what we can do and when, to help ourselves. When I asked my Instagram followers if they feel able to turn to their coping strategies when depression first strikes, most said they 'weren't sure' or that they sometimes need to wait it out a while. Many said they find it hard to identify it as depression at first, rather than 'feeling not right', so taking action becomes tricky. So, if like me, it takes you time to dig out your cape, that's normal – but I promise you it is there, waiting for you.

Depression won't go away on its own, this much I know. We absolutely can be the ones to challenge it ourselves (a thought that I find empowering and sometimes a little daunting), but timing and pacing are important – which is why we need the right plan, pitched at the right level for us, at the right time. We are the only ones who can climb out of our depression hole, but others can certainly give us a leg up. As with everything in this rather mind-boggling game, we deserve our own compassion and patience along the way – feeling better takes bravery and resilience, and that is deeply admirable.

Knowing our triggers: When should we kick-start The Plan?

Recognizing that we're tripping and stumbling our way down into depression's bottomless pit is something that I, and many others, find difficult. When I asked my social media followers how easy they find it to notice depression's arrival, they said:

* 'It takes me weeks to realize.'

* 'I'll know that something is happening, but it takes me a while to label it.'
* 'I'm only able to recognize it with the help of my therapist.'

Personally, I know that I feel different, maybe even 'not right', but I just think the fact of the matter is that I'm a piece of shit. I usually won't recognize it as depression until I've recovered, so you can imagine how easy I find 'catching it early'.

While not easy to sniff out depression's tediously unimaginative warning signs, it is possible to improve at this (and I know plenty of people who can call their low mood out for exactly what it is at the time). It doesn't happen overnight. I, perhaps like you, am still on that journey – but we can all get better at it.

The optimum time to shut depression down is AS EARLY AS POSSIBLE. The screamy capital letters are there to stress importance, not to frighten you. All we can hope to do is the best we can, with the knowledge and experience we have, and the tools and support available to us. Within those parameters, I'd like us to be able to dive into The Plan when we first notice that flat feeling, that withdrawal from life, which spells depression. As such, knowing our triggers – or signs that we need to kick into action – becomes monumentally important.

What should we be looking out for? How do we notice depression when it tries to cover its back with its silly lies ('You're just a shit person')? I have a couple of key tools.

Support crew klaxon

My friends and family – those I count among my 'support crew' – are usually the first to notice and voice that something's up with me. While my depression is busy trying to convince me that 'I've always been the worst person in the world', a text from my friend Tash will come in: *You've been quiet. Is everything alright?* (She knows it's not but sometimes a 'softly softly' approach is better than getting the bulldozer out.) That is my support crew klaxon – a blast of noise from the people who know me best.

Those moments feel horrible – either because I feel as if I've been caught out, or I worry that the situation is worse than I let myself believe. If others are noticing, it usually means things aren't as they should be, which can be scary but is also very handy. Why not try proactively embedding this into your Plan Ecosystem? Ask people you trust to be direct with you whenever they're worried you're not feeling right, so you can think about it – and even start on The Plan – together? Most people will value the chance to help when needed, and if you're actually okay and they needn't worry, you can feel relieved about that together!

When we think about catching depression 'AS EARLY AS POSSIBLE' this is unique to us – my personal 'as early as possible' is when my friends sound the klaxon, I don the cape and give The Plan a flappy-flap. That is what feels like my first opportunity to call out depression, so this is my aim, and I'd encourage you to make a mental note of yours.

Self-monitoring magical-ness

Not all of us are lucky enough to have a support crew that knows us inside out, or a support crew at all. Fear not, we have an equally great tool in our toolkit – our ability to 'self-monitor'. That is, reviewing and analysing our behaviour (as though we were an outsider looking in on our life) and deciding if anything we notice might be a warning sign.

As part of that, we might set certain thresholds or 'standards' that we easily meet when we're feeling good – things like how often we get to the gym, make healthy weekday meals or see friends. Dip below these and that's when our self-monitoring comes into its own. Rather than trying to convince ourselves that it's nothing more than 'feeling a bit odd', we're able to call this behaviour out for what it really is: depression's sneaky ways creeping in.

We'll do a deep dive into self-monitoring and spotting depression's signs in Chapter 10. For now, I simply want to stress the importance of being aware of our own behaviours and introduce you to the idea that we really can be our own best warning system to help keep depression at bay. We're magical like that.

* * *

The blare of our support crew klaxon and a sprinkling of that self-monitoring magic are incomparably powerful tools to help identify triggers that prompt us to 'don the cape' and kick-start The Plan. That takes time and practice – remember, depression has been doing its boring old dance for millennia, while we're comparatively new to it. Seven depression shimmies behind me, I still miss some signs all the time, but I also notice others sooner than I used to. Please grant yourself the gifts of grace and patience; we are improving, whether we see it or not, and we're on the right path.

Taking the tiniest of steps

Embarking on the start of our recovery journey can feel like standing at the bottom of a towering peak we're about to climb, wondering if we should have done a bit of training after all. Depression makes us feel incapable of doing most things, so this monumental task hardly seems fair.

It's time to turn that mountain into a molehill, so we can stomp our way right up that peak, cape billowing in the wind, like the depression-busting superheroes we can be. By breaking down tasks that feel 'too big', we reduce initial barriers and help ourselves take small steps towards a much bigger goal.

If, for example, you would like to start or restart an exercise routine, the idea of leaping back into the buzzy, crowded, high-energy group exercise class you used to do may seem impossible (I know people who'd feel daunted by that environment even when feeling good!).

If you're struggling to get out the front door at all, you might break it down like this:

* Day 1 – put your trainers by the door; perhaps try them on and walk up and down.
* Day 2 – go for a short, brisk walk that feels manageable and remember how it feels to push your heart rate up a little. You may repeat this for a week, perhaps walking a little further or faster over time.
* Day 8 (a week later) – take a visit to your gym (in your workout gear!), with a friend if it feels easier. Pop in and look around to familiarize yourself with the setting and equipment.
* Day 9 – try a short 20-minute workout. Do whatever you need to make it feel more doable. Arranging to go with a friend can be great motivation, or picking a quiet gym might make the experience feel less daunting.
* Finally – you might do that for a couple of weeks or months, before you feel ready to try that group exercise class you've been missing. It will still feel nerve-racking, but when you feel you could *maybe* try it, that's the time to jump in!

These are just some ideas; you know yourself best and what feels possible. It's incredible you're doing this at all, so do it to your own timescale and in a way that feels best to you – there is no rush. All the while, remember that your Depression Comfort Zone is there to be stepped out of. It's important we're mindful of pushing those boundaries when we can.

I know that The Plan can feel overwhelming but, once we learn the simple effectiveness of its ways, I promise that it can also feel reassuring. For me, the sense that we can be active agents in our recovery journey is a deeply empowering one – it really has transformed my life and my confidence. I hope that by understanding your triggers and then taking the tiniest of steps towards your goals, you will feel empowered too.

* CHAPTER 8 *

Assembling Your Support Crew

The Support Network Training Campus

It's the first day of term and there's a line of people snaking round the building – new, eager students, keenly waiting to enrol in this year's classes. Taking another look down the line, you suddenly realize, 'I know a load of them! Mum, Dad, my sister, my best friend, my partner, my ex, my lovely neighbour...even my manager at work?!' Whether you knew it or not, these are your 'support crew' – your support network – ready to start at the Support Network Training Campus, a place of learning for anyone who needs to, has needed to, or will need to support someone's mental health.

The campus is open to all – and thank goodness. For the people who love and care for us, depression is also tough but in a different way. They want nothing more than for us to feel better, yet often feel powerless themselves, unsure of how to help. So, understandably, the classes at the Support Network Training Campus are in high demand. Your most prized people know that you deserve to feel okay and they would do anything to help make that a reality.

If you've supported, or are currently supporting, someone struggling with their mental health, I'd first like to say – thank you. No 'thank you' will ever feel enough, but I want you to know how incredible you are. Support for someone can come in many guises: calling them when you get a minute; popping round every day; arranging their online shop; talking through the hard stuff; or just making them a cup of tea when you can (my fellow Brits will know that tea makes everything better). If you're unsure whether you're supporting someone, just 'being there' for an individual who's struggling with their mental health makes you part of their support crew (and an absolute saint).

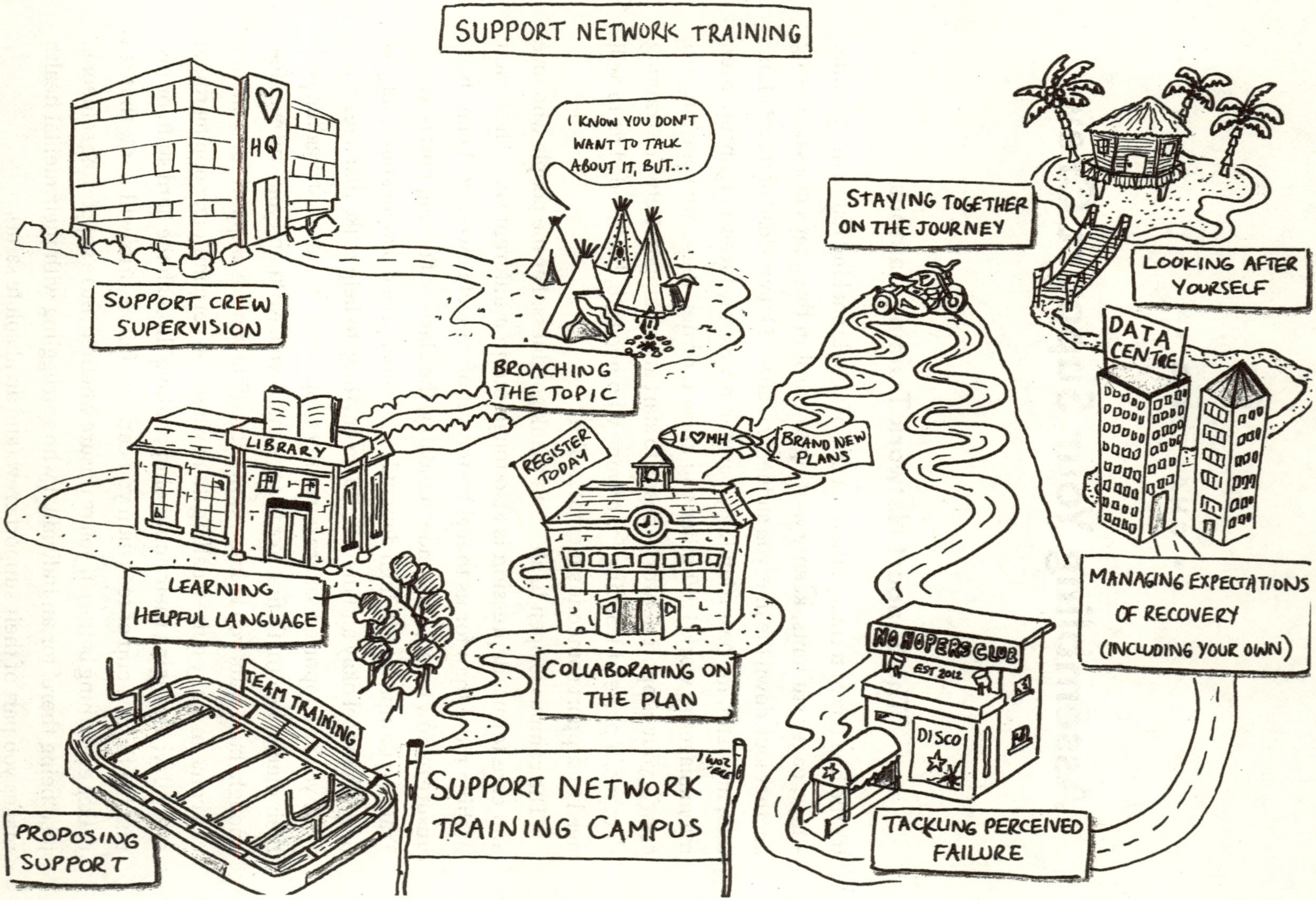
SUPPORT NETWORK TRAINING
HQ
SUPPORT CREW SUPERVISION
I KNOW YOU DON'T WANT TO TALK ABOUT IT, BUT...
BROACHING THE TOPIC
STAYING TOGETHER ON THE JOURNEY
LOOKING AFTER YOURSELF
DATA CENTRE
LIBRARY
LEARNING HELPFUL LANGUAGE
REGISTER TODAY
I ♥ MH
BRAND NEW PLANS
COLLABORATING ON THE PLAN
MANAGING EXPECTATIONS OF RECOVERY (INCLUDING YOUR OWN)
TEAM TRAINING
PROPOSING SUPPORT
SUPPORT NETWORK TRAINING CAMPUS
NO HOPERS CLUB
EST 2012
DISCO
TACKLING PERCEIVED FAILURE

Whether you're supporting someone or looking to your support crew for help, knowing what will help can be tricky. Everyone needs a little guidance, and those of us with our 'depression experience' are the best people for that job. Surprise! You're head lecturer at your own Support Network Training Campus! We don't automatically get a doctorate in supporting someone simply because we've been depressed, but we understand ourselves best and are uniquely placed to communicate our needs and what feels helpful. We can curate our own 'syllabus', choosing the right classes and course material for us and our support crew. We may not feel completely certain of our needs, or what will help, but never has a 'trial and error' approach been more apt - we're simply giving this a go together and working out what feels right.

Before we proceed - it's at this point that our Depression Voice is almost certain to pipe up, telling us that we're a burden on others, maybe even that they'd be better off without us, and we don't deserve anyone's support. I'd like to gently remind you that depression has no idea what it's going on about - you are wonderful, you deserve these relationships and your support crew want nothing more than to parachute in and help because they care about you.

Recruiting new sign-ups: Finding your support crew

Not everyone will feel that they have an obvious support crew. There are infinite reasons for this - social bonds can be hard to form and maintain at the best of times, and even more so if your circumstances make it difficult (e.g. a single parent working two jobs; someone who doesn't feel accepted by their community; re-location for work or personal reasons). Depression is exceptionally good at reducing our social circles, too, as we'll often find ourselves pulling away from human connection. If you've felt low for a long time, it's understandable - common, even - for your friendships and relationships to have dwindled and perhaps even petered out.

You are not alone - countless people move house, start afresh or need to rebuild their lives in some capacity, and will be looking to connect with new people. While we as depression masters may have an extra hurdle to overcome, as we won't feel our most confident or our 'full selves', the various available avenues for meeting others give us a great opportunity to try exercising that social muscle again and to gradually build our confidence.

Support – and the love and care held within that – exists in a wonderfully diverse range of guises. The best news is (and you may need to press mute on that Depression Voice to believe me for this next bit), new sign-ups can be recruited at any time. I have found that the beautiful variety of support offered by new connections can lead to some of the most brilliant, diverse and robust support crews around.

Back to that Depression Voice – it's probably going to tell you that there's no point trying to meet new people, that no one is going to like you anyway, that no one is like you and you won't have anything in common. So, I'd like to pose the idea of simply testing a hypothesis (just in case depression is wrong – p.s. it is).

These are some of the avenues where you might just meet a member of your support crew (and you may even become part of theirs!):

* Hobby, sports, or shared interest groups (e.g. a writing circle, knitting group, sports team).
* Volunteering opportunities (people volunteer for incredibly diverse reasons, so you might meet someone who 'gets' your circumstances).
* Charities and organizations that offer (mental health) support groups.
* Community action groups (e.g. litter picking at your local park – more fun than it might sound!).
* Classes and workshops (e.g. art, writing, learning languages).

These are just a few ideas. In researching this, I searched online for 'depression groups in London' and discovered so many options, both online and in-person, that you'd be spoilt for choice of ways to meet others in a safe, open and supportive environment (I share where to find examples, at the back of the book).

This can be a daunting prospect at any time – when our mental health feels stable, let alone when down a depression hole – so go easy on yourself if this feels like a mammoth task. Remember, there's no pressure; you're not expected to meet your brand-new besties for life and certainly not straightaway. Instead, view this as an opportunity to practise building relationships in a low-stakes environment. Joining a football club during my last depression spell was perfect for me. I got to hang out with a bunch of new people, who had no preconceived ideas about me, and engage in light conversation (or just bark orders at my new friends about where to stand on the pitch), while feeling closer to others. These women have been some of my greatest friends and supports ever since.

Support crews may start as a small thread of connection, which can strengthen, as fondness and care for one another develop. It's not weird or odd to feel that you don't already have an obvious pool of people to turn to, especially if your mood has been low for a long time. However, it's never too late to start recruiting into your support crew – trust me, I've been in those very shoes.

For our support crew: Let's get training

If you are supporting, or hoping to support, someone who's lurking down a mental health hole, this next part is for you – though it's useful for anyone. Welcome to day one of your training at the Support Network Training Campus – it's time for your course induction!

We'll cover some key, helpful topics here, to get you started. It's not about 'right' and 'wrong' support, but finding out what works for whoever you're supporting, and these tips should point you in a good direction. Onwards from here, it's consistency and open communication that will help develop your learning and understanding. Remember, you're not alone; there are infinite numbers of students enrolled in this course – so let's get training, together.

SUPPORT CREW TRAINING: CORE LEARNING MODULE

At the Campus, there's a core learning module, with a handful of top tips that are highly valuable for every student. If you're part of a support crew, looking for ideas, try starting with these key learning points that I've picked up through my own and others' experiences. This also works if you're looking for support yourself and wondering what advice to give your loved ones.

1. Be unconditional in your support

It's easy to feel as if the world has abandoned you when feeling low. In the nicest way possible way, tell the person you're supporting that they have it wrong. You could say something like, 'I'm here for you and I'm not going anywhere', and demonstrate that by being dependable and reliable.

2. Show up

Show up physically, verbally, however you want to. So long as you're there with your love and care. Try not to be absent during this time and be sure you can commit to something if you say you're going to do it (of course, sometimes life gets in the way, and that is understandable). Consistency and reliability really are key.

3. Let them know that 'the door is always open'

You need the person you're supporting to know that no matter how things have been, you're there for them, whenever they're ready. That goes for if they've ignored you, or engaged with you minimally, since they've been feeling down. None of that matters; your door is always open and they only need to step back through to pick right up where you left off.

4. Send the double text (my personal favourite!)

When someone has been feeling too low to respond to your messages or answer your phone calls, it can feel like a personal rejection or that your help is unwanted. The number one rule is: it is not personal. I genuinely wouldn't have responded to the Queen, had she texted me when I was at my lowest. It's not about you – this is just how they are currently engaging with the world.

If your text has gone unanswered for a couple of days, send a second text (the double), or go wild and make it a third or fourth if weeks have passed. Even if it's simply, *Hey again, you okay?* Or, it could be, *I know you may not feel up to talking, but I wanted you to know I'm here whenever you're ready.* Receiving a text, even when we don't feel we can respond, lets us know that people still care and counters the Depression Voice that will otherwise convince us that we're totally unloveable.

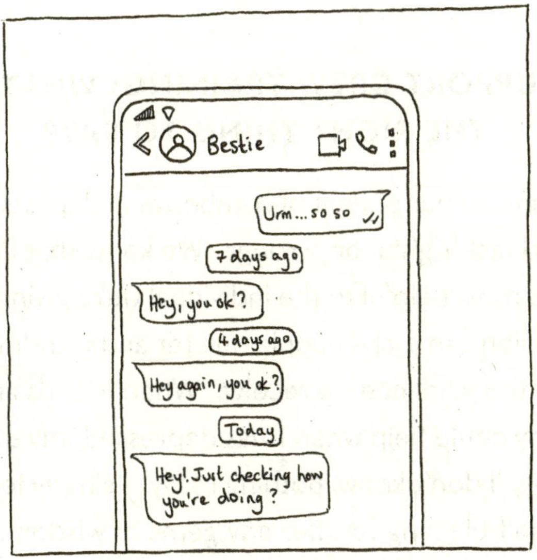

I'll be honest – supporting anyone through depression can be one of the toughest jobs going. There will be countless times when it seems hopeless. You can feel as if you're flailing around without a clue what to do and catastrophically failing. As someone who has felt the huge benefit of the simple *Hey again, you okay?* text (which I ignored on repeat!), my plea is that you keep going with your support in a way that feels manageable for you. Oh, and did I mention that you're a saint?

* * *

I've shared my top tips and I urge you to get your support crew enrolled in this module to learn them. But, ultimately, only you – as the person experiencing the low mood – can truly know the best way for your crew to support you. Communicating this can feel like a big responsibility when you're struggling through depression itself. That's why it's a great idea to run your Support Networking Training Campus (which – I'll say it! – is just a fictional campus to represent how we can communicate our support needs) when things are feeling lighter or when depression isn't hanging around. With a little bit of prior preparation and guidance, the next time depression dares show up your support crew can feel more confidently primed. Of course, every head lecturer needs some time off. Signposting your crew to online resources is also great, and I've provided some links at the back of the book.

SUPPORT CREW TRAINING: WHAT'S THE RIGHT THING TO SAY?

An ongoing theme in our pursuit of bamboozling depression is that there are no hard and fast 'rights' or 'wrongs'. We know that the best support is one that feels most helpful to the individual we're giving a helping hand to – but depression can make people quieter and withdrawn from reality, which can limit the guidance we receive. When friends and family would ask me how they could help when I was depressed, my ever-so-insightful reply was always, 'I don't know, nothing really.' I simply felt too hopeless, confused and self-blaming to offer any gems of wisdom.

One of the most common questions I get asked is what to say (and do) to best support someone. The language we use can be extremely powerful – in a helpful and, unfortunately, unhelpful way. Thankfully, I've developed a Support Crew Phrasebook to help with that. Imagine you've just landed in Spain and your one Spanish phrase of 'una cerveza, por favor' doesn't quite feel as if it will cut the mustard. The Support Crew Phrasebook can be your starting point, to teach you a few phrases, so you can feel more confident in communicating your support well in various scenarios.

You'll know that the only thing that any fully-fledged support crew member wants to do is to help someone feel better than they currently do. The Support Crew Phrasebook is there to give you some ideas for how to effectively, and compassionately, communicate that. It also gives us an idea of language to avoid – such language will usually be driven by good intentions, and a desire to see real change, but simply isn't landing in the right way. You can also ask someone you're supporting what they find helpful to hear. Ultimately, at the centre of it all is a relationship between two people. As this develops and you better understand one another, your combined knowledge will be better than any phrasebook I could ever hope to write.

The Support Crew Phrasebook			
Scenario	**What you want to communicate**	**Try saying...**	**Avoid...**
Offering your support (including if someone hasn't been replying to your texts or answering your calls).	You realize they're feeling low, and you'd like to help them in the best way to suit their needs (whether you've spoken recently or not).	'I've noticed you seem low/not yourself...' 'I want you to know that I'm here for you – now or whenever you're ready.' 'We can work out what support I can give that feels helpful.' 'I care about you, so I want to help. Even if you feel as though it's too much of a burden – it's not.'	'I want to help fix you/make you better.' (This suggests they are 'broken' or need to be 'made better' – instead, focus on *feeling* better.)
Suggesting working on The Plan together.	Having a plan could help them feel better, and you'd like to help them put one together.	'It's easy to feel directionless, lost or stuck when feeling low – a plan can lay out a path forward and provide structure, to counter some of these feelings. I'd like to help you with that, if you'd be open to it.' 'There are things we can do that could improve our mood; putting them into a plan is a good way of giving them a go in a way that feels manageable... How do you feel about trying it with me?' 'These things are always better done with someone else. Could we try making a plan together?'	'You *need* a plan – it will tell you what you *have to* do to feel better.' (This creates a sense of obligation, is overly prescriptive and removes that person's agency or choice.) 'I'm going to make a plan for you because I know it's helpful.' (This forces The Plan on someone, not allowing room for their participation.) 'A plan is great for accountability – I'll make sure you stick to it...' (This creates a sense of rigidity and expectations around completing The Plan. Accountability is a great perk of The Plan, but it's important not to make someone feel too beholden to an inflexible plan – they might feel like a failure if they don't meet expectations.)

cont.

Scenario	What you want to communicate	Try saying...	Avoid...
Encouraging someone to engage with The Plan in a more helpful way.	The Plan needs to be pitched right; we can't be too far in, or outside, our Depression Comfort Zone. It might be time to change their approach.	'I've noticed that you're doing really well managing things lately; do you feel ready to try adding in an extra plan or two in the week? It might help you feel that bit better.' 'I've noticed that you've been finding going to the gym difficult. That's okay – shall we review The Plan and see if we can replace it with something that feels helpful yet manageable?'	'You're not doing enough; you should be doing more.' 'You said you'd see a friend this week and you haven't. There's no point having a plan if you're not going to stick to it.' (This shames them or makes them feel as if they're underachieving. It creates a sense of obligation. Instead, focus on modifying The Plan to make it more appropriate.
Dealing with a particularly low patch (which they might assess negatively).	Having a particularly grim day/week/month doesn't mean they've failed – and you're here to help.	'Dips are inevitable and happen to everyone – it doesn't mean you've failed'.' 'Things will change, maybe a little, maybe a lot. But this isn't forever – it's just a tough patch.' 'I'm here for you regardless. Please feel you can come to me when things feel particularly challenging.'	'You were so much better last week – what's happened?' (This blames them for the change – asking 'if anything has changed for them' is a more helpful and supportive prompt to understand if their circumstances have changed and how you can help.) 'If you just did this... you'd feel better.' (This gives a sense that doing the wrong thing has created this dip.)
Encouraging someone not to give up (even if they think they already have).	Feeling as if you've given up, or want to give up, doesn't mean they have to – these feelings are normal.	'It is so normal to feel as if you've failed and want to give up; everyone does at some point, but I believe in you.' 'Has anything specific happened to make you feel like this? Perhaps we can talk it through.' 'The way I see it, you've been trying so hard; I really see all the progress you've been making, even if you can't.'	'Don't give up so easily!' (This makes them feel like a failure for feeling that they want to give up or suggests that if they tried harder, they wouldn't be in this situation.)

SUPPORT CREW TRAINING: YOU'RE HELPING MORE THAN YOU KNOW

As a student of the Support Network Training Campus, you'll be pleased to know that there is no final assessment or exam where you're scored on the support you give. You get 'top marks' just for showing up and being a constant in their life when they most need help. Have I mentioned, it even qualifies you for a sainthood?

There will always be limiting factors to the support you can give – and so there should be. Never has the aeroplane analogy, 'fit your own oxygen mask before helping others', been truer. As supports and aides, we need to look after ourselves to be able to care for those around us. Other life priorities, such as family, work, our own mental health and important responsibilities, should never be completely neglected in the process. Nor does 'being there for someone' mean having unlimited time, emotional capacity, or energy to help. We should be aiming to support within the parameters that we can, set at a level that feels sustainable. Some days, that might be dropping everything to be there for a friend, partner, or sibling; on others, it might be a text to say, *Thinking of you. How are you feeling today?*

I can guarantee that there'll be times when you feel that you're not doing enough, or even failing, as you support someone through a tough time. Instead, please know that your efforts are wonderful and there is no hierarchy of support. You are doing what you can and helping more than you know.

Perfect support doesn't exist

I have always felt so grateful for any help I've received in hauling myself out of my many depression holes – even, and especially, the *Hey again, you okay?* text. That said, there are also friends and people who I thought were part of my support crew that I felt let down by. It is okay to feel disappointed by the actions of some. Memories of friends who ended our friendship during or after depression decided to take a starring role in my life, or the close friends who didn't reach out when I fell off the face of the earth, feel saddening. I have never expected anyone to support me when going through the depression wringer, but it can still feel upsetting to feel forgotten, abandoned, or unsupported.

However, it allows us to truly appreciate those who do show up – these people are like gold dust and of immense value. If they have good intentions and try, that is paramount – even if they don't always get it completely spot on. At least one person will say what feels like the 'wrong' thing, without meaning to (special mention goes to, 'You don't look that depressed' – I'm sorry my face doesn't reflect the size of the hole I'm languishing in right now). It may be a case of something they said not landing right with you, some words feeling better or worse based on our experiences and our perspective. I've had experience of someone close to me unintentionally saying things that felt hurtful, but I realize that frustration, upset and stress can cause lapses in judgement. It didn't mean they weren't trying their best, nor did it invalidate all the amazing support they gave me before and afterwards.

We are not obliged to 'educate' anyone on how to support us or how to say helpful things. However, if you feel up to it, guiding others can really work in our, and our support crew's, favour. Most people simply want to do a good job but often don't know where to start. A planned conversation with our support crew in which you cover some ground rules or guidelines, especially if you know you have certain triggers, may remove some uncertainty for all parties, while also providing a moment of connection and 'teamwork'.

It's all about deciding what feels good to you, then ensuring that your biggest supporters have an idea of what that looks and sounds like. But be mindful that your support crew aren't therapists and your 'stuff' is layered on top of all their other life trials and tribulations; their capacity isn't limitless. Your support crew deserve a medal for trying their best and you deserve a knighthood just for making it through the day. It is more than enough – in fact, it's fantastic – that you and your support crew show up at all. (Support crew: I hear that sainthood applications take 7–12 working days to process – it'll be with you soon.)

Involving your support crew

You've got your kickass crew of support buddies trained up and on standby. They've left behind their Freshers' Week hangovers and they're here, rejuvenated and ready.

As depression likes to pretend the whole world has abandoned us, you may not believe that there is a support crew waiting for you at all. You could be surrounded by an army of loving fans, and you'd think they're a baying mob, furious that you still haven't replied to their texts. Depression fills our normal lives with silence and emptiness, while doing its shouty negative thing, muting the love and support that still surrounds us.

Even when we know that we're surrounded by people who'd support us, given half the chance, we may not feel able to ask them for help. You'll know me by now – I feel incapable of saying, 'I'm depressed', and following that with, 'And I'm going to need your help', feels incomprehensibly impossible. But that is exactly what my therapist would get me to do, prompting me to compose texts to my friends:

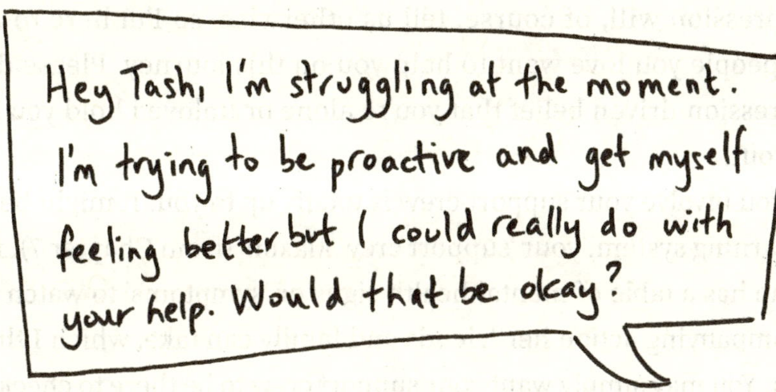

My therapist sat next to me as I hit 'send' (it was a good job she did, as that is the kind of tough task that I'd procrastinate over until it 'went away', i.e. never got done). It feels hard because mental health issues can feel shameful or embarrassing and asking for help, especially for something as complicated and persistent as depression, feels as if we're placing an imposition on others (even if none of this is true!).

Tash replied to my text, straightaway:

Tash is spectacularly wonderful, but, even so, this sort of reply is not unique to her. If we're lucky, we'll have people around us who love us, and a defining feature of any loving relationship is a desire to help and support the person we love. Whether depressed, anxious, manic, totally withdrawn, self-sabotaging, or any other state they might find us in, none of that affects their wish to help. Depression will, of course, tell us otherwise, so I'm here to remind you: the people you love want to help you on this journey. Please don't let your depression-driven belief that you're alone or unloved hold you back in reaching out.

How you involve your support crew is totally up to you. It might be as part of your warning system, your 'support crew klaxon' (from Chapter 7). I have a friend who has a table of mental health signs or 'symptoms' to watch out for, with accompanying action her friends and family can take, which I think is a great idea. You may simply want your support crew to be there to check-in regularly, or, you may want to sit down with them and work on your Plan together. There really is no one way to give or receive support, nor to communicate your needs. Most importantly, you should aim to pick the support that feels most effective for you. If it's helping propel you forward in your onward journey, that is perfect.

I have done depression without telling my closest confidantes – and I did manage to haul myself through that dingy quagmire and out the other side. But I have never felt so alone. We need cheerleaders to keep us going when the going gets tough. Instead, all I had was my own negative mental tape, stuck on a nauseating loop, telling me I was a total failure and would be like this forever. I needed my friends with their belief in me and a positivity that I couldn't find in myself, to pierce through those thick walls that depression builds, and to let in even just a sliver of light – and when I eventually told them, that's exactly what they did. That ability they have is nothing short of magical and I believe in it fully. I'm working on leaning into it more when I'm feeling down. If you can, too, please do.

The power of connecting with friends (not fish)

Low mood has many of us longing for solitariness: to be lost at sea in a dinghy, with only the fish for friends, sounds perfect to a depressed me. The reality is that human contact and connection – and, crucially, support – are much better for us than a school of mute fish. In fact, I think they are essential. Research shows that recovery from depression is easier for those who perceive themselves to have social support and feel part of social groups.[6] In short, it's really good for us to be with friends, however we feel. Making sure we keep the social connections alive that we once treasured, and will enjoy again one day, can make all the difference in supporting our recovery.

I must confess, when a depressed me turns up, all that theory goes down the drain. The 'me' that comes with a side of depression doesn't want to do anything with her friends and she *certainly* doesn't want to accept their efforts to help (my definition of hell, unfortunately). A non-depressed me can understand this: it is nigh-on impossible, feeling as I do when depressed, to consider friends turning up to badger me into, for example, joining them for a supposedly 'pleasant' walk and a coffee as 'helping in recovery'. I'll feel certain that I won't be getting better this time ('this is just what I'm like now') and everything is totally and utterly pointless. There's no point sitting across from a friend over coffee, your insides bubbling with anxiety and self-loathing, to supposedly help you recover from being the awful person you've become forever more. Right? Except, this is false, and there is a very good point to it all.

I won't dress it up: those meetups with friends always felt terrible (until one day they didn't). I sat there, feeling awkwardness exude from me, ashamed that I'd ignored them for so long and embarrassed that they'd felt the need to turn up unannounced to cajole me into some semblance of conversation. Meanwhile, my depression was certain that they were having an awful time: 'See, you really are shit to be around. Do yourself a favour and don't do this again – ever.' Making ourselves do things we don't want to do when gripped by depression will not instantly disprove all our fears, in fact it might confirm them, at first: it will probably seem pointless and unenjoyable, just as expected. However, let's remember the facts: this is just our mood talking. Every encounter with a true friend is good for us, and it *is* possible to feel differently if we keep at it.

One of my most vivid memories of a friend coming to shoehorn me out the door went like this. It was a normal day in my depressed life, and I was lying prostrate on the sofa, watching endless daytime TV, when my best friend, Karlia, turned up at my parents' house, where I'd been living since things had got tough. She breezed into the room and, with her characteristically bright and warm manner that brims with love, suggested that we drive to the petrol station and get an ice cream. I love ice cream (I can take or leave a petrol station) but my initial thought was, 'Ice cream! Yum. Hmmm, I could force myself to...but... do I really want to? No, I don't.' Despite this, ten minutes later, I found myself parked up by a petrol pump, with my best mate, eating Magnum ice creams, the scent of petrol fumes wafting in the background. I had made myself do it – and I was enjoying it.

We will never want to go for the petrol station ice cream when feeling low. In fact, it was the pressure of having my dear friend, looking at me with hopeful eyes, that twisted my arm into seeing it through. There will never be a day that, when truly in depression's clutches, I think 'Hell yeah!' to being with my friends. That is the effect of depression. We feel too awful about ourselves, too unloveable, unworthy, unlikable, too convinced that this unrecognizable version of ourselves 'is just what I'm like now', too bereft of hope, too far away from our love for life, too certain that nothing will lift the paralysing numbness we feel. I cannot see past the pain I feel in those moments. Seeing our friends, family or extended peer networks can feel like an absurd horror movie narrative being crafted before our eyes – and we're in the starring role. Terrifying. Not only does it all feel totally pointless, but the idea of accepting the love and generosity of another, when your own self-hatred is all-consuming and the thought of loving yourself makes you feel sick, is truly the stuff of nightmares.

However, we all wake up from nightmares. Most things in life are temporary – that is one of the things I find most reassuring about the human condition – especially feelings and emotions, and often depression. Getting support from others – even if just the petrol station ice cream and a joke that has you smiling for the first time in weeks – will probably feel uncomfortable and unwanted when depression is telling you that you're unworthy or are making it all up. But it won't always be that way. To get closer to this you will need to do one thing: make yourself meet up with friends – or connect in a way that works for you – when you don't want to. Remember, recovery is a lot of making yourself do shit that you don't want to do.

You could say it sounds simple, but we know that it can feel far from easy. My gosh, I did not want to meet up with Karlia, Tash, or any of the other people who forced their way into my depression cave. Every time made me feel like more of a failure, more boring and unworthy of their bright, sparkling personalities, and more undeserving of their love and kindness. But it felt like that until it didn't. One day that fog started to lift, and I realized that my day had been made better for seeing a best friend. Telling them how I'd felt that week felt good and sharing even just a tiny bit felt good, too.

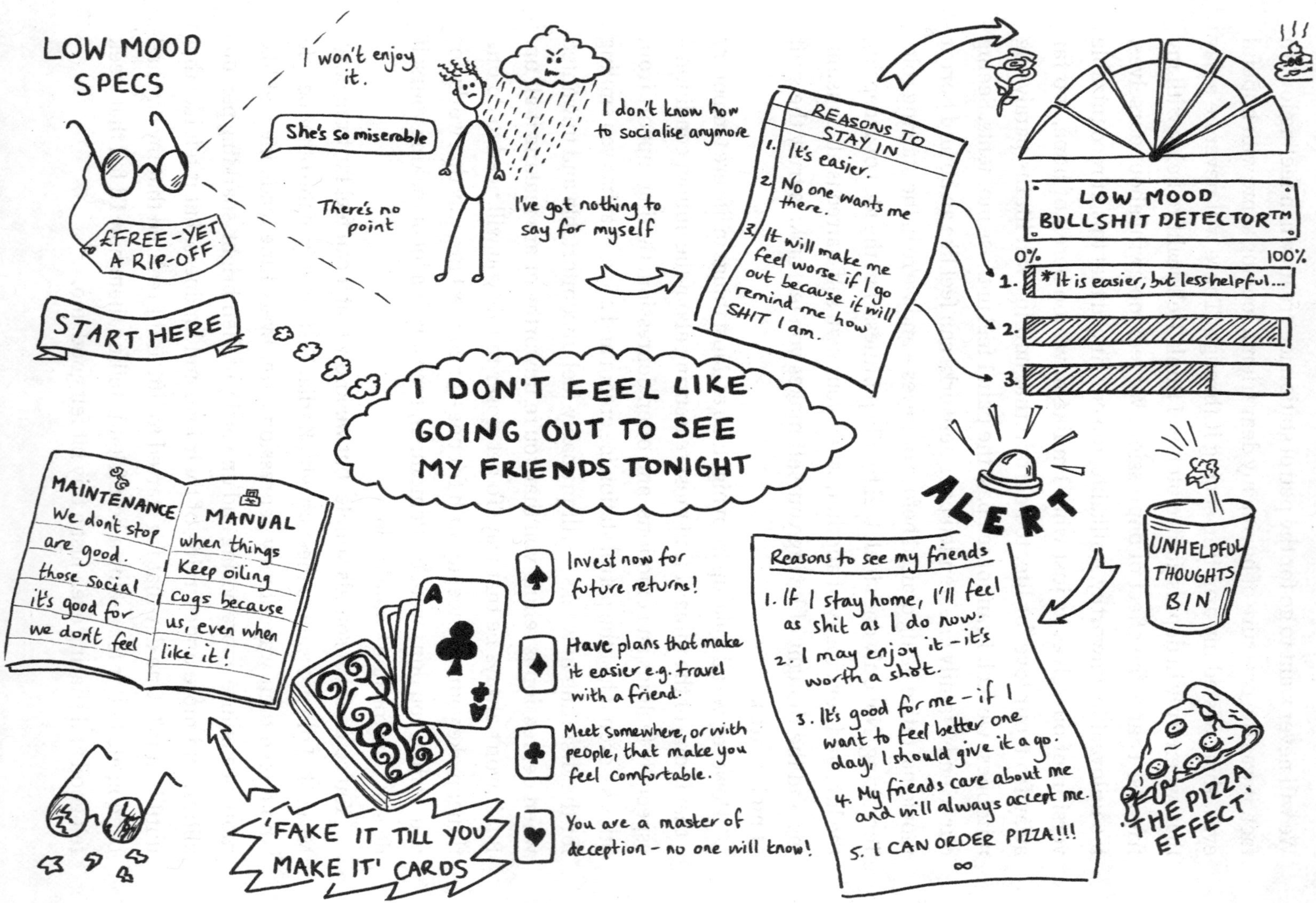
LOW MOOD SPECS
£FREE - YET A RIP-OFF
START HERE
I won't enjoy it.
She's so miserable
There's no point
I don't know how to socialise anymore
I've got nothing to say for myself
I DON'T FEEL LIKE GOING OUT TO SEE MY FRIENDS TONIGHT
REASONS TO STAY IN
1. It's easier.
2. No one wants me there.
3. It will make me feel worse if I go out because it will remind me how SHIT I am.
LOW MOOD BULLSHIT DETECTOR™
0%
100%
1. *It is easier, but less helpful...
2.
3.
ALERT
UNHELPFUL THOUGHTS BIN
Reasons to see my friends
1. If I stay home, I'll feel as shit as I do now.
2. I may enjoy it – it's worth a shot.
3. It's good for me – if I want to feel better one day, I should give it a go.
4. My friends care about me and will always accept me.
5. I CAN ORDER PIZZA!!!
∞
'THE PIZZA EFFECT'
MAINTENANCE MANUAL
We don't stop when things
are good. Keep oiling
those social cogs because
it's good for us, even when
we don't feel like it!
A
Invest now for future returns!
Have plans that make it easier e.g. travel with a friend.
Meet somewhere, or with people, that make you feel comfortable.
You are a master of deception – no one will know!
'FAKE IT TILL YOU MAKE IT' CARDS

If we let ourselves set sail in our depression dinghy, with only the fish for friends, we can't remind ourselves that love and support feel good. When depression is so good at making us our own worst enemy, we need that skill that friends and our peer network have in buckets: reminding us of the brilliantly positive qualities that we can't see in ourselves, especially when we feel low. They let us know that we are loved and deserving of that love. We are the person we always were, whatever depression tells us.

If you are fortunate to have some great friends, the very best thing you can do to piss off depression is to nurture those bonds (and remember, it's never too late to start assembling your depression support crew, if you feel you don't have those connections right now). Get them involved in your support crew, however feels helpful. It might simply be sending that WhatsApp reply that you've been putting off, even if just a few words, to get things going. I know how hard it feels, I really do. But you'll be surprised at the difference even that small bit of connection can make.

* CHAPTER 9 *

Stepping Inside the Therapy Room

Is therapy all it's cracked up to be?

Therapy changed my life. I will forever remember that initial session with my first therapist – it was the first time I'd connected with someone over my mental health. I walked in, confused, self-loathing and ashamed, still reeling from months of darkness. I wouldn't accept I'd been depressed; rather, I thought that I had 'royally messed up' my life. Leaving that session, those messy feelings didn't suddenly disappear (and it would still take me many months to call it 'depression'), but I carried something new with me. Hope. A little bundle of the stuff initially, but, with time, it would grow into my dependable sidekick – meet my Pet Hope! As I left that first session, I couldn't identify it as 'hope' just yet; all I knew was that I felt a piece of the 'old me' – the one that possessed self-belief and a fiery determination – begin to stir within and think about coming back to life. Week after week, as I returned to therapy, my hope grew larger (and so did my little sidekick!), gradually pushing out the confusion, self-hatred and fear that had taken up too much space for too long.

Therapy helped me make sense of an experience that once seemed totally unfathomable. My therapist was the only person to show me that those 'dark times' (as I was then calling it) were understandable within their context. Suddenly I could make sense of this previously mind-scrambling life event. Therapy has allowed me to rewrite my internal narrative, using knowledge and understanding. The effect of this has been a self-belief that I have learnt to nurture and grow myself, whether it's been two days or two years since I last had therapy. The benefits of therapy with a therapist who seemed to truly 'get me' have been constant and it's still my first therapist's voice I hear when I need to coax myself into more helpful behaviours. When I manage to treat myself with self-compassion, rather than beating myself up like nobody's business, it's often my most recent therapist's advice that pops into my head, reminding me to be kind to myself. Therapy has been instrumental in taking control of my own mental health, and continues to be, to this day.

Therapy isn't only about getting through low mood. One of the biggest surprises on this path has been how hard the 'stuff around depression' is, on top of dealing with the depression itself. It wallops great big dents into so many parts of our lives, leaving us running around, trying to patch them up. Therapy has helped me regain the confidence that deserted me, have difficult conversations with friends, process the loss of friendships and jobs, renegotiate my identity (in a positive way), rebuild my self-belief bit by bit, and so much more. It has given me what I like to call 'mental health confidence'.

As someone who has been depressed seven sassy times now, my confidence does not come from a guarantee that depression will never turn up again – I have had to accept that it might. Rather, our experiences of depression are so complex that confidence can come from some truly unexpected places. Therapy gave me a set of 'mental health truths' that form the basis of my confidence – and I'd encourage you to think about your own versions, whether they be found in or out of therapy.

MY MENTAL HEALTH TRUTHS

* I have agency in managing my mental health, understanding that I have the power, and ability, to affect change.
* I believe in my worth. I know that I am not broken, deficient, inferior, weak or bad, because of my depression.
* Depression isn't inevitable; it doesn't 'just happen to me', regardless of my circumstances.
* I can call on support, from my friends, family, therapist. I can look to these people, who will do what they can, with the tools they have, to help me.
* There is no right or wrong, and there's certainly no 'perfect'. I understand myself and my mental health better than ever before and I'm improving all the time.

These all equip me with confidence; from that foundation, hope truly can grow (just like my Pet Hope!). As is becoming clear, therapy is so much more than a bunch of useful tips and tricks to manage our mood. Whether I'm flourishing, at a bit of a low ebb, or struggling, it has helped me tackle life with more belief in my ability to manage, and regain control, when things feel as if they're slipping.

That is what therapy with a good therapist is. We can all pick up a cognitive behavioural therapy textbook or read the myriad books with exercises to supposedly 'retrain our brains' (if you sense cynicism there, you'd be right). Ultimately, we cannot help ourselves unless we understand ourselves, understand what has happened to us and believe in our ability to make change now. We can then layer any tools and coping mechanisms on top of that. Tools and strategies are important, but a great therapist will help you live with greater comfort, contentment and self-acceptance among all the messiness that depression often leaves behind.

My therapists' belief in me, when I haven't been able to find it myself, has been vital. So, first thing's first, I need you to start telling yourself (and believe!) what has been impressed on me in therapy:

* You're not a failure.
* Depression is not your fault.
* You absolutely can do this.

Is therapy right for me?

I believe that therapy is right for everyone, but not every therapist is 'right' for every individual. I don't believe in 'good' or 'bad' therapy, rather the 'fit', or how well suited you are to a particular therapist. There are also more types of therapy than I could ever hope to know – integrative, Gestalt, cognitive behavioural therapy, Jungian, behavioural, and dozens more. If you're in therapy already, but it doesn't feel right for you, you might not be suited to the type you're trying, so it's worth researching options to see what feels most useful (I've shared a useful link to the British Association for Counselling and Psychotherapy's list of therapy types at the back of the book).

Perhaps you don't feel you click or gel with the therapist(s) you've tried – that is a valid feeling. It has been shown that a good connection between therapist and client can lead to better outcomes.[7] You don't have to be besties, or think a night down the pub with them would be an absolute hoot, but if you've given it a good go and still don't feel it's working for you, trust your gut and try someone else. However, it's always worth giving a therapist a fair chance (unless it's alarm bells from the start); you'd be surprised how bonds can build and progress can be made over time.

Barriers to therapy: Social and cultural factors

Even if therapy is right for us, there are so many barriers to stepping inside the therapy room and having a successful therapeutic relationship. On top of long waiting lists and eye-wateringly expensive private therapy, culture- and gender-based barriers may play a part in how likely we are to try, or stick with, therapy.

Certain cultures, religions and community groups don't feel that therapy is a credible or viable treatment option or they might entirely reject the validity of 'mental health issues' and any associated treatments. Gender can come into it too. In a patriarchal society, there is even more pressure on men to 'hold it all together' and hide any sign of perceived 'weakness'. When the community around you might have particularly strong, and unfavourable, opinions about going to therapy (however brave you're being in doing so), it's understandable that you're unlikely to waltz into the nearest therapist's room, gleeful that you're indulging in this act of self-care. If you feel similar barriers to accessing therapy, it might be worth speaking to someone you trust to explore the idea, or even a charity that specializes in mental health support (I have included a list of useful organizations on my website, which you can find at the back of the book). It is tough but I'd like you to remember that we all deserve support, and therapy can be an excellent option.

A shared background can also create a deeper understanding between therapist and client. As a South Asian person, for example, having a therapist with a South Asian background may help you feel more comfortable sharing intimate details about your childhood and family life. It might also remove the need to explain relational dynamics and customs that, for example, a non-South Asian person is unlikely to have experienced. Similarly, members of the LGBTQIA+ community, neurodivergent people, or other minorities, may feel safer discussing their particular challenges with someone who 'gets it' through lived experience. While my first therapist wasn't queer, we were both north Londoners, both Jewish, and had a similar sense of humour – all things that contributed to a therapeutic relationship that felt like the right fit for me.

If starting on your therapy journey feels like too big a leap, for any of the reasons above or similar, please visit my website (details in the back of the book), where I recommend social and cultural-specific groups and resources. The appropriate support can make those barriers feel much less daunting.

Demystifying the first session: What you can expect

Booking and turning up to your first therapy session can be anxiety-provoking – more so if your friends and family haven't tried therapy and it's very much 'unchartered territory'. I was beside myself with nerves before my first session. But I needn't have been – this session (normally 50–60 minutes long) is generally an initial 'consultation'. It's a 'trial run' of sorts for you to figure out if therapy with this therapist feels like a good 'fit'. You don't need to worry about what you say in this first encounter (and it's even quite normal to feel as though you have nothing to say!) – think of it as simply a 'conversation' (which is what my therapist calls our time together, rather than a 'session' or 'appointment', which I really like). It is a collaborative two-way interaction, which will be led by the therapist.

While a first session will vary, depending on the topics you bring to therapy and how your therapist likes to work, you can expect some common elements:

* Discussion of how your therapist works with clients – they may have a document for you to read after the session that lays out their 'terms of engagement'.

* Decision-making on how you'll meet, if there are options – virtually or in person. Either works brilliantly, so just settle on a space that feels most effective for you.

* Decision-making on the cadence of your sessions – weekly/fortnightly/monthly? It's important not to feel pressured into the frequency – it should feel like a helpful rhythm for your needs.

* Discussion of why you're there – the therapist will probably ask questions to develop their understanding and to begin your exploration together.

That's about all there is time for in a first session – it'll fly by! The rest is for you and your therapist to co-create over time, as you get to know each other, the topics you wish to explore in more depth, and how you like to work together. Every therapeutic relationship is unique, and I still feel mine evolving all the time.

So, I encourage you to take the first step if you think you might benefit from therapy (and I believe everyone can!). Before you do, here's my top piece of advice: take the time to reflect on how you *feel* coming out of that first session. Therapy can, and often will, feel hard – that is to be expected. However, if you feel that a therapist has provided a safe space within which you see the potential for meaningful progress and growth, that is the very best sign there is.

What if therapy isn't available to me?

Unfortunately, too many people do not have access to the therapy they need. State-funded therapy may not be available, or waiting lists might be devastatingly long (and depression does a good enough job of devastating already, right?). Privately funded therapy, the other alternative, is prohibitively expensive for most people. A lack of access to therapy is a systemic issue that exists the world over. It's understandable to feel let down by the system, especially when mental and physical health services should be valued equally, but still aren't.

Despite such a vast deficit in accessible mental health provision, my deepest wish is for everyone to have the feeling of agency, power and support that therapy has given me and others. But therapy isn't the only option – we shouldn't underestimate the power of people and community.

You also now have this book. I wrote it with the belief that a mental healthcare system that doesn't adequately cater for all shouldn't prevent anyone from learning how to look after their own mental health. That said, this book is not a replacement for therapy. Certain things work best within the relationship developed inside the therapy room, and there is a reason that therapy can be transformative, especially when you're rolling around in depression's dank ditch. But I hope to pass on some of the material you might cover in a therapeutic setting, and that I have found extremely helpful.

Therapy is not the only option!

Therapy is only one part of this multi-faceted equation. There are so many support avenues that yield their own unique supportive superpowers – whether that be alongside, or instead of, therapy. Support can come in so many forms and guises, and from any source – it is anything that helps share the load, making those steps we take feel that much lighter, especially when times seem hard.

Our invaluable support crew have a huge part to play in this. While they may not be trained in the same way as a therapist, your closest friends and family provide a different kind of care – it's built on a special foundation of love and memories of you at your fullest and most vibrant. What's more, support isn't just about the hour spent in a therapy room. Your support crew can check-in with you regularly, help pick you up when they notice you're down, and provide a safe space in which to share.

If you're unsure of where, or who, to turn to, we've already explored some great options for building new connections. There are meetups and support groups to help guide you, and where you can meet people who have been, or are, exactly where you are now (you can find examples on my website and details are at the back of the book).

Ultimately, I want you to know that any support that you find helpful is valid, in whatever shape it comes, and I hope that you can get the support you need however feels best for you – because you really do deserve it. If you can find people with whom you can be honest, your true self, and can share with them without fear of judgement, that is the very best kind of support there is out there.

* CHAPTER 10 *

Self-Monitoring and Spotting the Signs

Self-monitoring: Working out if we're in, or headed towards, a hole

Depression transforms anyone's life. It comes along, tips it upside down, gives it a good old shake, returns it the right way up if you're lucky, but more often than not leaves your life scrambled up and teetering on the edge of a cliff. It then turns to you and says, 'There you go, over to you.' Thanks, Depression.

The difficulty in spotting depression is that we're not looking out for the life that has been left in shredded tatters on the edge of that cliff. We're not even looking out for a life that looks as though it's been dragged through a bush backwards. To spot depression in time, and to halt it in its tracks, we ideally want to pick up on the slightest sign of it lurking about. We need to get good at looking at what might seem like normality to the untrained eye, and then noticing the seams that are starting to fray and pull apart. Low mood and depression are much harder to beat once they've been given the time and space to bed in. They will try and creep past us inconspicuously, so we need to be attuned to even the slightest of signs.

This process of 'noticing' is what my therapist and I would call 'self-monitoring'. Self-monitoring is the act of taking a step back from ourselves, figuratively speaking, to gain distance from our thoughts, feelings and behaviours, so we can observe what's going on. We can then draw some conclusions about what we see from this new vantage point. They might only be hypotheses at this stage – a hunch that the evidence indicates something isn't quite right. In fact, reading back on my journal entries, written as I've been getting depressed, I report, 'I don't feel quite right.' That's all I'm able to pick up on. But that's all we need – a basis on which to assess if we need support or to employ our coping mechanisms, including getting out The Plan with a flamboyant flourish.

'Helpful' vs. 'unhelpful' self-monitoring

There's no doubt that self-monitoring forms a crucial part of staying well. In fact, the likelihood is that, if you're someone who has struggled through a period of low mood or depression, you'll naturally be self-assessing to a degree. The woman who was assaulted late at night while walking through a park will forever be more wary and alert when walking alone after dark. She'll be listening out for the slightest scuffle or disturbance of leaves because memory and trauma influence our present-day behaviour. Those of us who fear depression's return are likely to be similarly vigilant in different circumstances that feel triggering or 'risky' based on past experiences. I certainly am.

I'm also a living example of the concept of 'helpful' and 'unhelpful' self-monitoring.

One very average afternoon, I suddenly felt myself descend into a pit of panic and anxiety. I'd been playing recent events over in my head, doing my self-monitoring thing without even knowing it, performed a few complex mental health equations, and suddenly one plus one was equalling DEPRESSION. Sound the alarms! I sent a frantic text to my best friend, followed by a panicked email to my therapist, and flapped around my room, trying to think of a way I could stop the depression that I was convinced was quickly and efficiently taking hold of me. In that moment, I'd forgotten everything I knew about my mental health. I knew that depression doesn't descend on anyone in a mere moment – it is usually a slow but steady onset over many weeks, even months. I also knew that I need more than one sign in recent events, that has lasted for more than the one morning I'd used to carry out my assessment, to conclude that depression is knocking at my door.

I had over-monitored. 'Over-monitoring' is when our settings are out of whack and we're set to 'high alert', reading into normal situations to find signs of depression where they probably don't exist. This can be exhausting and creates a set of feelings – panic, fear, anxiety – that are almost always unhelpful. We need to monitor but not to the point that we're drawing erroneous conclusions that negatively impact our lives. A hard – but achievable – balance to strike.

When we over-monitor, our Over-Monitoring Monster comes careering into the room. A clumsy creature that is intimidatingly huge and powerful, while also incompetent and ineffectual (imagine a towering fluffball that constantly trips over its own feet); a beast that is never our best friend but does have the best of intentions. We've been so busy trying to look after, and protect, our mental health that sometimes we over-do it, normally from a place of fear. That's when our Over-Monitoring Monster comes striding in, with its commitment to total and utter panic, lack of rational thought and nonsensical conclusions. Unfortunately, the poor buffoon doesn't know how to do anything but shout and stomp around, raising the panic alarms night and day, which is a recipe for emotional and physical exhaustion.

I know that ferocious ball of fluff has good intentions, but we need to keep it locked up and under control. Instead, we'll be focusing on how we can self-monitor in a balanced, helpful and sustainable way. Our self-monitoring will help us take a step back and gain a more measured and objective view of the thoughts, feelings and behaviours we exhibit, to steer ourselves towards a more positive course of action. It will allow us to note when we're making something out of nothing but also when we're burying our head in the sand and ignoring the signs of low mood (my forte, as I'll soon explain!). Unfortunately for our Over-Monitoring Monster, for this to work, this must be an Over-Monitoring Free Zone. They'll be okay, though – I hear retirement is quite nice.

Unhelpful self-monitoring: Tried and tested approaches

Let's imagine we've self-monitored and we've realized that it's likely that depression is on its way over. It's holding a dead bunch of flowers, wearing its finest 'Eau de Self-Hatred' and it's crawling up your driveway, humming a hideous tune.

There are two types of behaviour that are natural – but polar opposite – examples of how we might respond to the prospect of depression darkening our doorstep. There's, 'Manning the panic stations' once we spot the slightest sign of our mood dipping – whether our assessment is an accurate one or not. There's also, 'Burying our head in the sand', because there's a lot less to worry about when your head is submerged in the ground so as not to notice anything – or it might seem that way. Believe it or not, neither of these is a response to self-monitoring that we want to aim for. 'Manning the panic stations' will mean we're hyper-vigilant and exhausted by constantly monitoring and reacting to the smallest sign of a dip in mood. Meanwhile, 'Burying our head in the sand' will render us oblivious to valid signs, allowing difficulties to build and become harder to eventually tackle. However, there is an aspirational middle ground! Simply named, 'Noticing and executing a plan'.

TRIED & TESTED RESPONSES TO SELF-MONITORING
AUTHOR-TESTED
MANNING THE PANIC STATIONS
PANIC
LOOKS LIKE: Hyper-vigilance; you'll be super sensitive to any perceived 'evidence' and may act from a place of fear. Much panic.
PROS: You feel like you're being proactive and avoiding things getting worse. It can feel safe.
CONS: Inaccurate, exhausting and likely to take its toll on your well-being in the long run.
SELF-MONITORING AND EXECUTING THE PLAN
THE PLAN
A
B
C
LOOKS LIKE: Working with a therapist or your support crew to make a plan that helps you challenge low mood, when you notice its tell-tale signs.
PROS: You will be reacting to realistic 'warning signs' in a helpful way, with people who can support you.
CONS: It's not easy and you'll feel outside your comfort zone. It will take time and practice – that's more than okay.
BURYING HEAD IN THE SAND
LOOKS LIKE: It's hard to tell; it's pretty dark down there... you'll push any worry about signs to the back of your mind and carry on as you are.
PROS: It's sort of peaceful in the dark. There's an initial relief and comfort in pretending everything is fine (but it doesn't last).
CONS: Low mood is given the space to settle in. You'll have to come up for air at some point and helping ourselves can be harder the longer it's left.

As an experienced 'head burier', it's taken me time to embrace noticing and executing any kind of plan; now if you so much as whisper, 'The Plan' to me, I feel all warm and tingly. Whether you're a panic stations manner or a head burier, you'll know about the simple power that The Plan can hold (from Chapter 5). Now we're learning when to spot the signs correctly, so we know when it's time to dust that masterpiece off and dive right in.

How to self-monitor in a helpful way

Let's go back to the analogy of the woman in the park. Unless we tackle our over-monitoring, going for a walk will never feel pleasant, feasible or positive. 'But this is what keeps me safe!' I hear you cry. It may feel that way, but we can tread the line between keeping the big clues in focus, while trying not to sweat the 'small stuff' (such as a down, anxious, or lethargic day, that reminds us of when our mood was last persistently low).

I've made this point already, but it's such an important one: very few people have a completely stable mood, energy or emotional state (in fact, I'm yet to meet such a person). There is a natural ebb and flow – impacted by hundreds of factors, including our experiences, surroundings, physical health, current stressors and the world at large – of how we feel on any given day. For some of us that might feel like more of a chaotic roller coaster than a ride on the teacups at the fairground, but everyone has their version of fluctuations in mood. While those times can be tough, it is normal to find some days more challenging, more anxiety-provoking, or simply harder work, whereas other days feel like a total breeze.

Instead of individual emotions or episodes, we need to monitor themes. We've met my Over-Monitoring Monster; you may recognize your own version of that big fluffball and we need to try our best not to pay attention to all the little things that they pick up on. For example, don't panic if you feel exhausted after the working week and can't face going to that school reunion to spend time with people who used to exacerbate your insecurities. A school reunion is many people's idea of hell – chalk this one up to having had a crappy week and not feeling up to putting yourself through it.

However, if you keep cancelling dates with friends, delaying (or missing) deadlines, postponing tasks (which might make you more stressed), regularly missing football training and calling in sick to work, then you really need to pay attention to this. This is not your Over-Monitoring Monster, this is helpful self-monitoring. It's tricky because there are no 'right' or 'wrong' amounts of activity we should be doing, and no perfect balance that should be struck between solitary activity and things you do with others – we are all different in terms of where we need that balance to lie to keep us operating at our baseline. Some people will relish an opportunity to head out in a big group and throw some moves on a sticky nightclub dance floor every week, while others would prefer a quiet drink every now and again and an early night. The key is understanding what is right for you and doing what you need to keep yourself 'ticking over' and feeling good.

We can use a checklist of 'changes' in behaviour to highlight significant shifts in mood that are worthy of our attention. Though it might seem counter-intuitive, the list below should be assessed in relation to you at your best. I know that, when feeling really bad, simply stopping your mood from languishing in the gutter feels like enough of a tall ask – why in tarnation am I asking you to compare yourself in your depression hole with your seemingly long-gone better self? It's important to remember that, regardless of how long you've been feeling low or depressed, you have the capacity to feel good – great, even! You may get back there, or you may end up somewhere slightly different. Either way, it's this version of you that should be your benchmark when trying to notice if your mood has started to slide. In this way, you can try and stop a downward trajectory as early as you can.

These are the sorts of changes you need to look at when self-monitoring:

1. Going out:

* What have I planned recently – is it less than usual, less than I want to be doing or less than others around me seem to do?
* Have I cancelled more things recently – do I use excuses of work deadlines or family parties to avoid people or places?
* Does being in public fill me with dread and doom?
* Does an invitation fill me with anxiety and a certainty that I/they won't enjoy the event or company?

* Do I find or make excuses not to see friends or family (even if they've asked to see me)?

2. Hobbies and activities

   * Have I stopped doing the things that I used to enjoy? Baking, walking, going to the cinema or the gym?
   * Have I thought about doing new things recently but dismissed the idea – predicting that it'll be too hard, I'll be no good or that I won't enjoy it?

3. Conversations

   * Have I stopped chatting to people with whom I come into contact where I live, work, volunteer?
   * Do I give short answers to questions that could be 'conversation starters' and not allow others to find out anything about me?

4. Lifestyle: sleep, diet, exercise

   * Have I stopped looking after myself like I used to? Am I eating less healthily, cooking less, exercising less, not having my hair cut or coloured regularly? Have I stopped wearing make-up or wearing my hair in the way I think suits me best?
   * Am I sleeping more or less than I used to? Am I practising good sleep hygiene or allowing myself to fall asleep on the sofa watching TV?

5. Relationships and sex

   * Have I stopped engaging in friendships and/or personal relationships?
   * If in a relationship, have I been avoiding sex or intimacy or lost any interest in them?
   * Am I avoiding intimacy (either sexual or emotional) and is this impacting on my relationship, if in one?
   * If single, have I stopped showing any interest in dating? For example, having a profile on a dating app, or considering myself too unworthy to date. (NB. As someone who has spent a lot of their adult life as a 'single

person', I know that the desire to date can wax and wane. Make sure that, if you're taking a break from dating, it's because it feels right to you, not because you believe that no one would want to be with you.)

6. Thinking about taking your own life

    * Have I been thinking that life just isn't worth living and that I would be better off dead? Have I been thinking about how I'd do it and perhaps researching it online? Have I made plans or started to think about how or when? (If so, please reach out to someone and get support. Things will get better, and although this feels like the only solution at the current time, it really isn't and there are better times ahead for you.)

If you have been low for a long time, it can be difficult to evaluate change, as your social circle and activity might have dwindled considerably. You may also have decided that this is right for you – perhaps it is, but there's a chance it isn't. You need to be very honest with yourself and consider whether this is really your preference for how you live your life or the product of a chronically low mood, low self-confidence and a lack of motivation. Thinking about how you'd like your life to be (attainable and realistic goals are great; it doesn't need to be a hugely lofty aim) rather than what you feel capable of right now can be a good exercise. It is likely that if you are feeling low, your mood has impacted your choices and, in turn, those choices are further impacting your mood. If this could be true for you, my suggestion is that it is time to experiment with change and see if this might help. The longer it has been, the more overwhelming making that change will feel, but even small adjustments make a difference. Going at your own pace is key.

The Self-Monitoring Majig

For helpful self-monitoring, we know that there is a balance to be struck. I want to introduce you to a handy bit of kit: the Self-Monitoring Majig. It's one of my depression defying devices. This one helps us notice signs we really need to pay attention to, so we can reach helpful, as-accurate-as-possible conclusions about our mood. Its balanced assessments stop our Over-Monitoring Monster coming out to play (sorry, buddy – today's not your day).

Into our Self-Monitoring Majig funnel goes 'life data' (thoughts, feelings, behaviours); they are processed in an advanced testing and analysis centre (our brains, making sense of it), to produce a final assessment – am I okay, depressed or getting depressed? The depression alarm will sound if (and only if) our final report spells out 'depression'.

Our Self-Monitoring Majig has a number of carefully calibrated settings and thresholds. Our job is to tweak them until the sensitivity is such that we're not calling on our Over-Monitoring Monster, nor missing low mood's warning signs all together. A good starting point would be to programme the list of 'changes' in the last section into that testing centre. We need to be looking out for a handful of persistent changes across the various categories I shared, because low mood tends to seep into multiple life domains (e.g. work and home life) and for at least two weeks. We can be flexible still, so if your assessment paints a picture of a life in which you're not coping, that's a sure enough sign as any.

This self-monitoring business is not easy. You will likely panic without cause, skip over depression staring you right in the face, and all the shades of grey in between, in your valiant efforts to get ahead of depression. Seven dalliances with depression in, I miss my low mood all the time – I'm clearly still fine-tuning my Majig's settings! It's important to go easy on ourselves, noting our successes, rather than the times low mood still manages to slink past unnoticed. Try, 'I noticed it eventually and got there in the end', or even, 'I noticed it a little earlier than last time.' If depression insists on being nasty to us, we can be our own gentle cheerleader, proud of the times we self-monitor as best we feel able to.

Spotting the signs early: Stopping the slide off the face of the earth

Depressed me doesn't believe in gravity all that much – that may seem bizarre, but hear me out. When I'm low, I feel as though I've slid off the face of the earth. Gravity has lost its hold on me, and I've gone a-slipping-and-a-sliding off this lump of rock and out into the solar system. No friends see me, no texts get replied to, no phone calls are answered, and I hide away at home. It comes from a deep desire, driven by depression, to disappear entirely (or at least we think so – it's unlikely to be what we really want). You may call this whatever you like – hiding, self-isolation, hibernation (remember, we can use whatever language feels most comfortable) – but I rather enjoy the drama of my 'slide off the face of the earth', which also feels accurate.

We slide off the face of the earth because of the urges that low mood brings. We can think of depression's job (that no one asked it to do) as protecting us from the outside world, which can feel overwhelming. We long for aloneness, silence and distance from others, and total inactivity. The 'slide' quickens as those behaviours become self-propelling. Inactivity leads to doing less and less, and isolation can lead to loneliness and a loss of confidence to socialize at all. My brand of depression sees me binge-watching daytime telly, just about dragging myself out for a walk (but through deserted fields where I won't be seen), and waiting interminable hours for the day to end, while dreading the dawn of a new day. My mood is maintained by stripping all opportunity for achievement or enjoyment from life, and so my slide off the face of this earth continues. You may be familiar with how it feels to 'disappear' like this too.

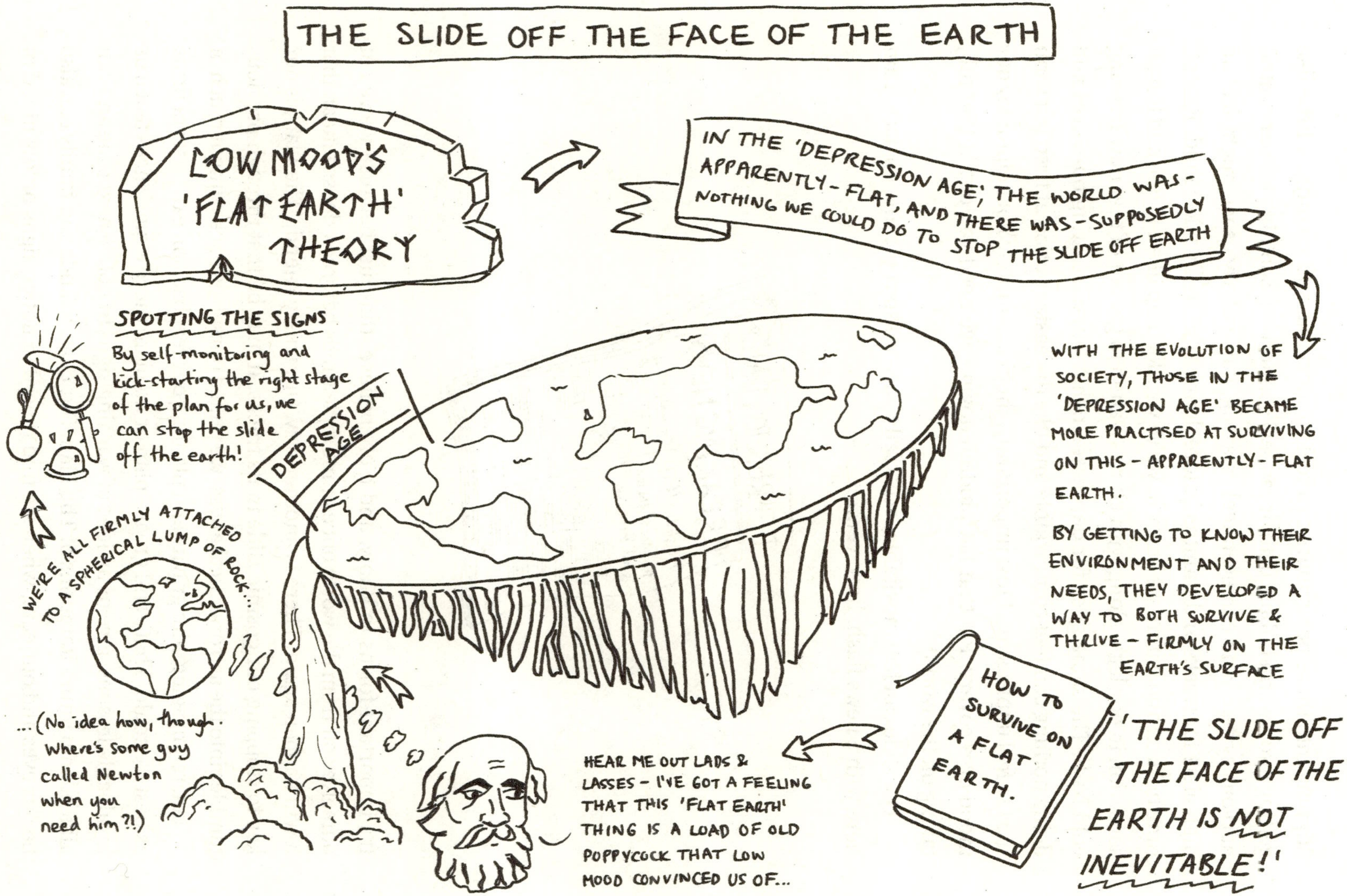
THE SLIDE OFF THE FACE OF THE EARTH
LOW MOOD'S 'FLAT EARTH' THEORY
IN THE 'DEPRESSION AGE', THE WORLD WAS - APPARENTLY - FLAT, AND THERE WAS - SUPPOSEDLY NOTHING WE COULD DO TO STOP THE SLIDE OFF EARTH
WITH THE EVOLUTION OF SOCIETY, THOSE IN THE 'DEPRESSION AGE' BECAME MORE PRACTISED AT SURVIVING ON THIS - APPARENTLY - FLAT EARTH.
BY GETTING TO KNOW THEIR ENVIRONMENT AND THEIR NEEDS, THEY DEVELOPED A WAY TO BOTH SURVIVE & THRIVE - FIRMLY ON THE EARTH'S SURFACE
HOW TO SURVIVE ON A FLAT EARTH.
'THE SLIDE OFF THE FACE OF THE EARTH IS NOT INEVITABLE!'
DEPRESSION AGE
HEAR ME OUT LADS & LASSES - I'VE GOT A FEELING THAT THIS 'FLAT EARTH' THING IS A LOAD OF OLD POPPYCOCK THAT LOW MOOD CONVINCED US OF...
WE'RE ALL FIRMLY ATTACHED TO A SPHERICAL LUMP OF ROCK...
...(No idea how, though. Where's some guy called Newton when you need him?!)
SPOTTING THE SIGNS
By self-monitoring and kick-starting the right stage of the plan for us, we can stop the slide off the earth!

Slipping into these behaviours can feel comfortable and inviting. A little like getting into a warm bubble bath, it can feel comforting, soothing for our central nervous system, and can even feel relaxing, particularly as we might feel on high alert for weeks and months before depression really takes hold. Except, time ticks on and before we know it, we've wrinkled-up like a prune and lost all sensation in our legs, along with all motivation to get out of that now freezing cold bath. The same goes for depressed behaviours; isolating ourselves and doing nothing can feel comfortable and like the easier option at first, but soon start to feel unpleasant. Most importantly, they're definitely not helpful for our mood or recovery. Put that bath loofah down – we need you out of that tub, taking on the world!

The slide can feel inevitable, especially once we start picking up pace. I am here with a news flash, however...

It's important for us to know, and truly believe, that just because we've cut ourselves off from the world once or multiple times before, it doesn't mean that it will happen again. There is another way. Our trusty friend, 'The Plan', is our key to stopping our cosmic slide in its tracks. It may be that through previous tumbles into the astronomical abyss, we pulled ourselves back without much of a plan, re-engaging with gravity and planting our feet back on earth's terra firma as best we could. That's still great – plan or no plan, these experiences teach us invaluable lessons, give us an idea of warning signs to notice next time and can all feed into future iterations of The Plan. Our close friends and family can also be our eyes and our ears, when we find it hard to notice signs of low mood in ourselves (or perhaps are indulging in a bit of avoidance). A plan shared helps split this responsibility and we can all pull together to prevent the slide.

The slide's origin story

To stop the slide off the face of the earth, it's helpful to know *why* it happens in the first place.

Isolation from the world is one of the easiest ways of ensuring that we don't have to engage with it any longer. Once you've got the basics in place, it's entirely self-sustaining. Cut off all contact with friends and many will stop 'bothering you'. Stop going out and you'll soon forget what was even good about it ('Fresh air? Who needs it!'). The reason we do it in the first place is driven by our low mood and the changes to our perceptions (explored in Chapter 2): we only see the negative, remember the negative and interpret things negatively, so this seemingly hostile world becomes a place to shelter ourselves from. If our brain is telling us we're too shit to be around, why would we want to put our friends or ourselves through that? If we're no longer able to feel enjoyment like we used to, why would we bother doing the things we used to enjoy? If we are to believe depression, the world is too shit and we are too much of a useless failure, so why bother engaging with any of it? The Plan's job, with the help of our support crew, is to get us pushing against this instinct to let ourselves slide off the earth, and to prove to ourselves that we are still the same person who can enjoy all the things we used to.

It has always seemed to me as if depression has descended on me in a flash, a 'blink and you'll miss it' moment. However, the reality is that depression usually takes a while to settle in. It tends to take its time before it's got its shoes off, cuppa in hand, and settled down in your brain. The lightning-fast part of the slide off the earth comes at the end, sending us catapulting out into the cosmos, as multiple factors come together and our mood can no longer take the strain. Our challenge is to try and notice the small slips along the way (unanswered texts, missed social events and gym classes) that build that momentum, so that we're not flung into outer space.

We're building a picture of the way that our mood and depression works – in phases. Those phases can't be predicted precisely – not in duration or intensity – but we can make a multi-phased plan to match the stage of the slide we find ourselves in. We can trigger the part of The Plan that matches the speed we're slipping at (and the types of behaviours we're engaging in), and hope that this will slow us down to a halt.

To start, we'll focus on a couple of scenarios we might face, where low mood is just starting to creep in and effect your day-to-day ('feeling a bit funny'), and when it's embedded itself such that you're finding it too hard to engage with life as you used to ('I don't care about anything').

'FEELING A BIT FUNNY'

You're feeling a bit 'funny'. Maybe it's low mood or maybe you're tired and having a rough week; you're not sure. Either way, you really don't want to go to the pub tonight, even though everyone is going. In fact, being around people has felt a little tough lately and you've found yourself to be quieter than normal. Still, exercise is your solace, as always – that hasn't changed – and you're enjoying the gym more than anything else.

Analysis

We've caught you at a good time, which is at the very beginning phase of the slide. You're still enjoying certain things, like going to the gym, but you're struggling with things you used to find easy, like socializing. At this stage, you could probably still make yourself go out with mates, even when you don't want to. So that's what The Plan will help you do.

'I DON'T CARE ABOUT ANYTHING'

Your friends haven't seen you in quite some time. You feel okay texting them, but you don't feel as if you've got anything to say, so you wouldn't put them through spending time with you. Exercise has gone out the window, to be replaced by sleeping in. In the evenings, you stay up till 2am, watching TV shows you don't really care about and eating junk food, which makes you feel worse about yourself. Your performance at work has declined, and you'll only work from home now – except, you don't really care and have no motivation.

Analysis

You're heading towards the speedy part of the slide and are teetering precariously close to the edge. You've stopped almost everything you used to enjoy, but you're doing well to keep in touch with friends a little, and you haven't stopped working. If we kick-start The Plan now, we have a chance of stopping your galactic slide in its tracks.

In both these examples, The Plan can help – but its focus or intensity will vary, depending on the situation. I've never met a depression hole The Plan can't help pull me out of, even when languishing in the deepest of pits, because of its infinite versatility. There is always room for incremental change, however small – our first goal is to simply get us feeling a little better, and hopefully closer to where we want to be eventually. It becomes trickier the longer we leave things. When depression is booming its soul-crushing put-downs through a megaphone, it takes all our energy just to keep going, let alone to do the hard stuff. By aiming to stop the slide as early as possible, we give ourselves the very best chance of implementing The Plan.

From everything to nothing

I've always been told I can be a bit of an 'all or nothing' type, but I didn't know just how true this was until I met my old pal depression. When down in depression's swampy depths, my diary or calendar was as bare as they come. I remember distinctly that, in my busiest week, I had one lonely doctor's appointment (and I stressed for days about getting out of the house to go to that). Plans disappeared from my diary in unison with my mood sinking, and my weeks, and my diary, became progressively emptier and emptier.

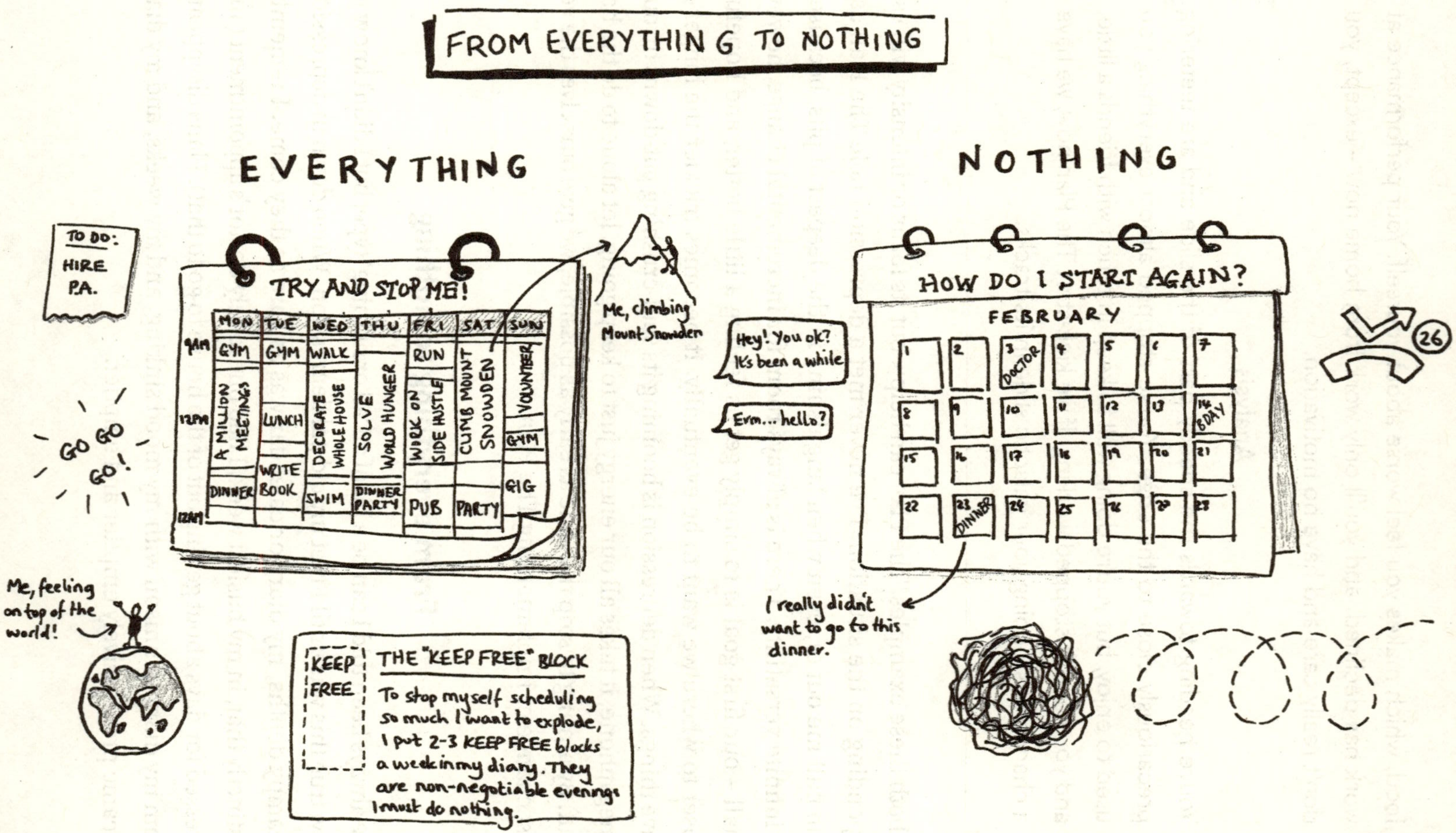
FROM EVERYTHING TO NOTHING
EVERYTHING
TO DO: HIRE P.A.
TRY AND STOP ME!
MON TUE WED THU FRI SAT SUN
9AM 12PM 12AM
GYM GYM WALK RUN VOLUNTEER
A MILLION MEETINGS
LUNCH
DECORATE WHOLE HOUSE
SOLVE WORLD HUNGER
WORK ON SIDE HUSTLE
CLIMB MOUNT SNOWDEN
GYM
WRITE BOOK
DINNER SWIM DINNER PARTY PUB PARTY GIG
GO GO GO!
Me, climbing Mount Snowden
Me, feeling on top of the world!
KEEP FREE
THE "KEEP FREE" BLOCK
To stop myself scheduling so much I want to explode, I put 2-3 KEEP FREE blocks a week in my diary. They are non-negotiable evenings I must do nothing.
NOTHING
Hey! You ok? It's been a while
Erm... hello?
HOW DO I START AGAIN?
FEBRUARY
DOCTOR
BDAY
DINNER
26
I really didn't want to go to this dinner.

When my diary wasn't eerily quiet, it was often head-splittingly noisy and full. My unhelpful recovery trait is that, once recovered, I'd cram in as much as possible – maybe I was trying to get as far away from the sofa-ridden 'me' as was possible. My diary would be bursting at the seams, running me ragged. At times, I've buckled under the pressure of a heaving diary, overwhelming me and running me into the ground – unfortunately, often leading to low mood once again.

Reflecting on the shifts in my diary with me, you can see how the state of our diary could be a good indication of our mood. Knowing this, we can include it in our toolbox of useful tools, helping us to analyse our mood (especially when our head is telling us, 'Everything is fine, just keep going'), reflect on how we're looking after ourselves and consider that it might be time to give The Plan a good shake-down and get cracking.

What might doing too little tell us about our mood? It could be that we feel we aren't good enough to be around people, or that we don't enjoy the things we used to (so why bother), or that we don't have the energy needed to plan and then get out and interact with the world. All these things point to low mood slowly stealing us away from our full life.

What might an overly full (and perhaps stressful) diary tell us about how we're looking after ourselves? It's likely that we're living our life unsustainably – and, as with everything when it comes to mental health, we're aiming for sustainability and steadiness. When my diary is crammed to the rafters, it may only be a matter of time before I become overwhelmed, balls start dropping, I feel as if I'm failing to keep up and the slow descent into doing too little, or nothing at all, might begin. My therapist and I would call this 'squeezing 48 hours into 24' and I now know it can be a precursor for my slippery slide off the face of the earth.

We all have different life thresholds and parameters. Many of us will have a diary as steady and reliable as the tides – perhaps you're more of a home body, or enjoy a healthy work, gym, socializing routine – and are unlikely to see wild fluctuations. In which case, you might not notice much of a shift in your living patterns when your mood is low. Our diaries can still be useful, but we'll be looking out for smaller changes, such as, am I socializing only once a week now, instead of twice, and am I dreading it whereas before I didn't? Or have I ordered more than one takeaway a week lately because I'm not bothered enough to cook healthy meals? It can be helpful to quantify these changes to get an accurate picture.

There is 'no one size fits all'. We all have different styles of engaging with the outside world. In psychology, this is explained by the Sociopathy – Autonomy Scale. People who display more 'sociotropy' invest more in interpersonal relationships; those who demonstrate more 'autonomy' are more independent and self-determined. We are all somewhere on this spectrum, and how much time spent socializing or being around others feels manageable or enjoyable will be dictated by our natural leanings. When thinking about our activity levels, we should work within these.

I have traditionally found it hard to notice when the balance isn't quite right – getting swept up in a busy high or ignoring a glaringly quiet low period. Meanwhile, I know that an outsider could easily draw an accurate conclusion, if they were to so much as glance at my calendar. In fact, I often benefit from getting that external perspective. Cue my therapist shouting 'cut', 'cancel' or 'reschedule' as I would show her my diary bursting at the seams. At other times, she'd survey the barren desert that was my diary, pointing out that one doctor's appointment does not constitute a plan for the day, and push me to add in more. You don't need a therapist for this – members of your support crew could easily step in. My friends have often approached me to say 'Jacs, we've not seen you in months; do you fancy getting some dates in the diary?' These are great examples of working in tandem with our support crew for mental health maintenance. It might even help us to independently monitor and reflect on our own diary more objectively in the day-to-day, as we practise viewing our diaries through the eyes of a friend.

Whatever works for you is perfect. I would recommend considering using your diary as one part of your mood barometer and making changes to your activity schedule (from Chapter 5) to get your mood moving in the right direction.

* CHAPTER 11 *

Detecting Low Mood's Bullsh*t

You are stronger than depression

When we're in the thick of it, depression can feel extremely hard to beat. We'll often feel as if we're wading through a depression-y bog, getting tangled up in the weeds, spectacularly face-planting in the sludgy water and having to pick up our bedraggled selves time and time again. Experience has taught me that it's the 'getting back up' that builds our courage and confidence, as we prove to ourselves that we're able to find our way through the messy bits regardless. Still, depression will have all of us feeling helpless at times. So, it's time I let you in on a few truths about its supposed strengths (psst, it's not half as strong as it would have you think).

First, I know how powerless we can feel to depression. Most times that depression has turned up in its skimpy Gladiator outfit, showing off its silly biceps, I've felt frozen to the spot. A torrent of unrelenting negative thoughts about ourselves and the world around us – presented as 'facts' to us by our mood – feel inescapably big and loud. By contrast, we're likely to feel small, vulnerable and meek, and it can feel as though all we can do is to give in to depression's *perceived* (this word is important!) power and strength, as it becomes the only backdrop to life we really remember.

It's understandable, in that case, that we often provide depression with circumstances in which it can thrive, unchallenged. Taking helpful steps can feel anywhere from hard to impossible, believing ourselves incapable or that any efforts would be futile. Plus, life seems pointless anyway – so what's the use in trying? We've explored how inaction breeds further inaction; before we know it, we're responding to depression with, 'Okay, I won't shower or leave the house, if you say so. While I'm at it, I might as well stop texting friends back too, right?' Using a good bit of activity scheduling (from Chapter 5), we know we can take away the 'nothingness' that depression demands, and reclaim that space, gradually filling it with everything that makes us who we are (or, right now, we feel we 'used to be'). We have so much more power than low mood will let us realize, and believing in our own strength can help us bulldoze through depression and its tricks.

Depression can be a big old liar

Once we realize that depression's strength is based on lies, trickery and duplicity, we can start to learn its trademark techniques and catch it out. It hasn't bothered to evolve, so its assertions – that you're shit, useless, worthless – remain unchanged. We've heard all its passé slurs before, which makes it that bit easier to spot them and trample over them. We won't catch it first time every time, and if you're still convinced by depression's lies sometimes, join the club! It really is a case of practising and learning more about ourselves and our mood as we go.

The thing we always need to hold front of mind – especially when depressed – is that depression can be a big old liar. Unfortunately for us, those lies are indiscriminate and persistent, regardless of the counterevidence we have that undermines their validity. Let's take a look at a couple of depression's classic lies to get us going.

The facts:
You wrote your friend a lovely birthday card and took them out for a special birthday meal (even though it felt tough because you felt low).

Depression's lie:
'Call that being a good friend? You're so uninventive and uncaring, you might as well not have bothered. Do her a favour and give up on being her friend now.'

The facts:
You've been working hard at your job and making a real impact in your work (even though depression has sapped all your energy).

Depression's lie:
'You're so terrible at your job and so unproductive that someone's bound to notice. I wouldn't be surprised if you got fired soon, you fraud.'

These are the more nuanced, well-thought-through lies that depression can tell us. Check out this list of its favourite, totally unimaginative ones:

* You're worthless.
* You're useless.
* You're a waste of space.
* You're shit.
* You're rubbish.
* You're lazy.
* You're selfish.
* You're ugly.
* You're unloveable.
* You're unworthy.

Annoyingly, depression's voice can be deafening, so – despite knowing what we do about its lies – it becomes very hard to challenge that voice with a more truthful narrative. However, it's not impossible, and you really can a) acknowledge those assertions for what they are: unfounded slurs; and b) work on replacing depression's negativity with a more neutral perspective – and eventually a positive one, when you can muster it! I'm going to start you off on this journey with a big, juicy truth: you are still the same person as you were before depression came stomping into your life. You've simply lost sight of your many great qualities. You believe these nasty things of yourself *because* you are depressed; you aren't feeling low because you *are* those things at all – a hugely important distinction.

Soon, I'll take you through some ways to execute a judo-like flip on depression's lies. But, before we start, I need you to know that you won't believe the counter-arguments and balanced suggestions you first try to make. You may not even believe that depression is lying. Whenever I'm depressed, I always seem to take out a membership for the 'I'm the biggest piece of shit alive' club, sometimes for months on end. If we think back to the cognitive model in Chapter 2, we'll remember that when our mood is low, we notice the negative, remember the negative, and interpret things negatively. Our Depression Voice feeds off and survives on that stuff. Therefore, while you might not believe the small voice in your head, as it tries to remind you of your true worth, psychology shows that there's a high likelihood that there's another, less negative, side to the story – and a much more valid one than any old rubbish depression trots out.

Not only does depression churn out lie after lie, for many of us, it also has the audacity to pretend it's not there at all. A little-known fact: depression is the undefeated 'Hide & Seek' Champion of all time, and here's its trick. Immediately after booming, 'You're a useless piece of shit' through a megaphone, or whispering 'Go on, give up, you failure' in your ear, it jumps behind that bush in your garden, letting you think that *you're* the issue. As you're left checking unenthusiastically behind the curtains (still the best hiding spot of all time), only to realize no one's there, you seem to have no choice but to believe that these thoughts are truths and come from you. Instead, we need to nurture a new belief, that they are nothing more than the lies of a mind that depression has set up camp in. You need to nurture a new belief, that they are nothing more than the lies of a mind that depression has set up camp in.

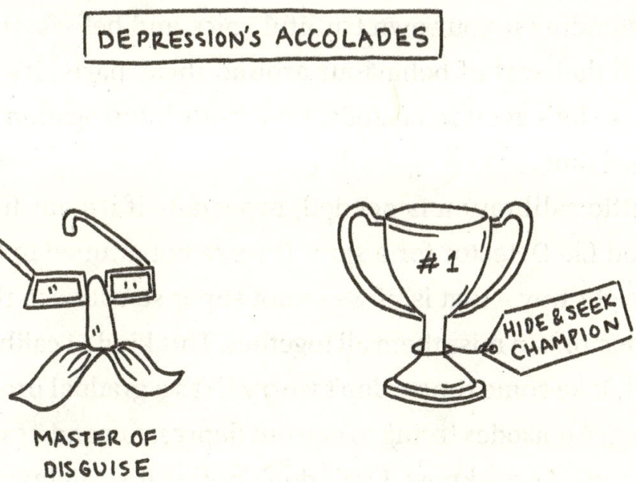

Knowing that depression can be a big old liar, we have a basis from which to start challenging its authority and its supposed power. When we combine this understanding with our very own alert system – 'WARNING! DEPRESSION LIE!' – we stand a chance at beating depression at its own game. It takes time and practice to develop this, but you can begin right now by training yourself up to catch out, and counter, depression's untruths.

Introducing the Low Mood Bullshit Detector™

Allow me to introduce you to my pioneering piece of trusty kit that'll help us get wise to depression's trickery. Welcoming this depression season's must-have gizmo: the Low Mood Bullshit Detector™ (also available as a multi-buy bundle with the Self-Monitoring Majig). This handy contraption lives in our brains (including yours!) – so no last-minute online shopping orders are required. So far, we've taken a whistle-stop tour of the lazy lies that depression tells us about ourselves; with our shiny new toy, we'll be learning to call out that steaming, smelly bullshit long before we step in the stuff.

Stage 1: The Low Mood Lie Detector

There are three parts to our Low Mood Bullshit gadgetry. First up, it's the *Low Mood Lie Detector* – this helps us notice low mood's lies in the first place. It's here that we catch out anything that could be depression, drowning us in negativity and then pretending it's our own truthful voice and beliefs. Depression can't get away with that sort of behaviour around these parts; it's time to hold it accountable, so let's get it in custody, under our interrogation lamp and start giving it a hard time.

First, a little calibration is needed, especially if it's our first time taking our Low Mood Lie Detector for a spin. If we're not attuned to low mood's lies in quite the right way – that is, if we're not super sensitive to them – our Low Mood Lie Detector can miss them all together. This kind of calibration can, and probably will, take some time – don't worry if it's a gradual process. I've spent seven depressive episodes trying to call out depression and its nasty negativity when it turns up. As we know, I still don't notice it straightaway, or I miss it entirely, but I feel proud that I continue to tweak the settings on my Low Mood Lie Detector and see improvements over time. As we become more dialled into the voice in our head and what it's telling us, we'll start to see lies where we once thought there were truths – would you just look at those wild spikes on your Low Mood Lie Detector report!

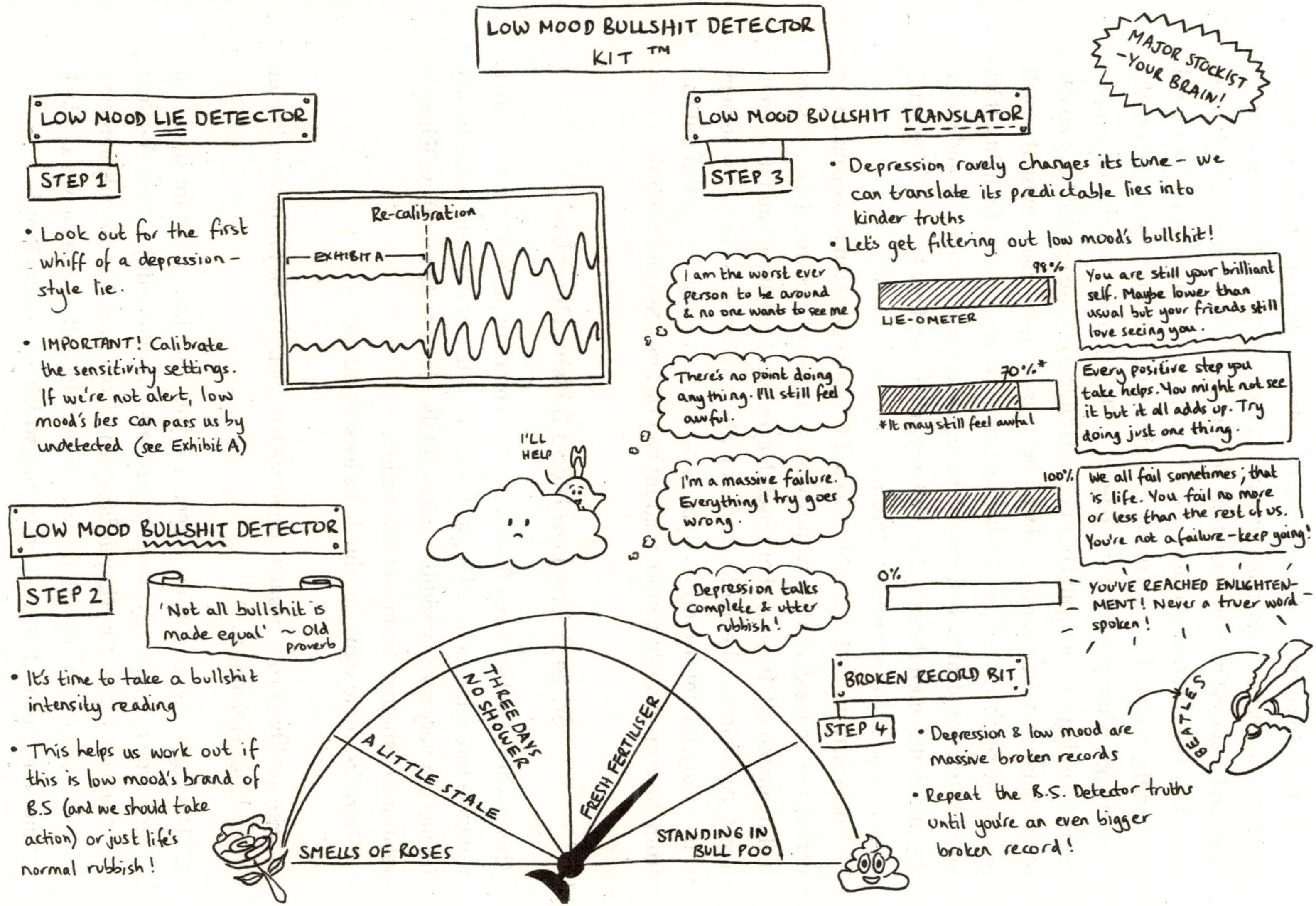
LOW MOOD BULLSHIT DETECTOR KIT ™
MAJOR STOCKIST – YOUR BRAIN!
LOW MOOD LIE DETECTOR
STEP 1
• Look out for the first whiff of a depression-style lie.
• IMPORTANT! Calibrate the sensitivity settings. If we're not alert, low mood's lies can pass us by undetected (see Exhibit A)
Re-calibration
EXHIBIT A
LOW MOOD BULLSHIT DETECTOR
STEP 2
'Not all bullshit is made equal' ~ Old proverb
• It's time to take a bullshit intensity reading
• This helps us work out if this is low mood's brand of B.S (and we should take action) or just life's normal rubbish!
SMELLS OF ROSES
A LITTLE STALE
THREE DAYS NO SHOWER
FRESH FERTILISER
STANDING IN BULL POO
I'LL HELP
LOW MOOD BULLSHIT TRANSLATOR
STEP 3
• Depression rarely changes its tune – we can translate its predictable lies into kinder truths
• Let's get filtering out low mood's bullshit!
I am the worst ever person to be around & no one wants to see me
98%
LIE-OMETER
You are still your brilliant self. Maybe lower than usual but your friends still love seeing you.
There's no point doing anything. I'll still feel awful.
70%*
*It may still feel awful
Every positive step you take helps. You might not see it but it all adds up. Try doing just one thing.
I'm a massive failure. Everything I try goes wrong.
100%
We all fail sometimes; that is life. You fail no more or less than the rest of us. You're not a failure – keep going!
Depression talks complete & utter rubbish!
0%
YOU'VE REACHED ENLIGHTENMENT! Never a truer word spoken!
BROKEN RECORD BIT
STEP 4
• Depression & low mood are massive broken records
• Repeat the B.S. Detector truths until you're an even bigger broken record!
BEATLES

We need to consider the negative thoughts swirling around in our heads in relation to our own normal inner critic. We all have a self-critical internal voice and it doesn't have to mean that we've bought a one-way ticket to Depression-ville. That internal narrative, even when negative, can be part of a normal and healthy range of human thoughts and feelings about ourselves – but, like most things, when practised in moderation. To differentiate between depression's steaming cow dung and our normal inner critic, we need to keep an eye on the balance. When our mental well-being is in a good place, most of us will have some semblance of balance between negative and positive thoughts. If it's out of kilter, significantly in favour of the negative, that's when we should notice it – and that's when those spikes will appear on our Low Mood Lie Detector report for us to pay attention to (gosh, it's a useful bit of kit).

That's why it's best to double check if this is depression jabbering on, or perhaps we've just had a few crappy weeks – the kind that would have anyone feeling pissed off, frustrated or upset. Maybe we're exhausted and in need of a rest. Positivity can be hard to come by when we have no energy. Nose pegs at the ready, it's time to sort low mood's particularly pungent brand of bullshit from the ever-so-slightly more fragrant Eau De Life's Normal Rubbish.

Stage 2: The Low Mood Bullshit Detector

This is where the *Low Mood Bullshit Detector* comes in. If we feed our negative thoughts into our machine's sophisticated testing and analysis centre (really it's just our very own incredible brain – all the kit we truly need!), we'll have a reading on whether we should take action.

Here are some signs you should be looking out for:

1. The quality of your negative thoughts has changed; they're nastier, louder and more relentless.

2. The negative thoughts are directed at you, with little room for shades of grey: you're *totally* ugly, *completely* useless, the *most* selfish person *ever*, and *utterly* worthless. Or, 'They *definitely* can't stand you and are only agreeing to see you out of pity' (all-or-nothing thinking, otherwise known as 'black and white' or 'dichotomous' thinking, which depression loves!).

3. These negative thoughts often have no evidence to support them; they're not necessarily precipitated by a particular event or a demonstration of the traits you're chastising yourself for.

4. You can't seem to rationalize these thoughts or counter them with a more balanced, realistic view of yourself. This is depression's bread and butter – stubborn, biased negativity – and therefore particularly important to notice!

I don't believe in strict criteria for assessing our mental health, or how we feel – we are complex beings, blessed with the capacity for infinite variety. So, I'll leave the inflexible perspectives and sweeping generalizations to the psychiatrists responsible for the *Diagnostic and Statistical Manual of Mental Disorders* or *International Classification of Diseases* – manuals used by clinicians to categorize and diagnose mental health issues. However, if you find that most of the qualities above ring true for your own self-talk lately, it's likely that your mental health could do with some TLC to get you to a better place. Luckily for us, it's this kind of thinking that our Low Mood Bullshit Detector will be calling a resounding 'BULLSHIT!' on, so we can start to make a plan.

Our new alert system isn't there to cause alarm. I'm not suggesting any of us pull my favourite move: at the first sign of depression, throwing my hands in the air to exclaim, 'Well, that's it, here we go again! I'm done for. The world order is collapsing, the universe is caving in on itself, and my life as I know it is over. I can be nothing but a passive bystander to my inevitable demise.' Instead, noticing unhelpful thoughts (helpful self-monitoring), acknowledging that this is low mood's nasty language rather than our own, and using them as a sign that we're struggling, are key elements of our survival strategy. Once we've noticed, we can begin charting a new course, aiming to avoid the turbulent waters that low mood steers us towards.

Back to our gadget. No need to be alarmed, but our Low Mood Bullshit Detector report has identified that depressed thoughts are in the building (or brain, to be more precise). Now we're aware, it might be that we start to piece together more evidence that we hadn't noticed previously. Have we been going out less? Have we felt more tired recently? Have we felt less motivated at work? Have we stopped enjoying things we used to love? As we know from Chapter 2, low mood has thought-based, behaviour-based, and physical symptoms. The chances are, if we're paying close attention, we'll start to see signs of depression's impact across all those realms.

Stage 3: The Low Mood Bullshit Translator

We've identified depression's bullshit, and our nostrils are full of its pungent smell. It's time to move on to our third and final piece of apparatus: using our *Low Mood Bullshit Translator* to turn depression's lies into truths. It's not magic – we need to roll our sleeves up, get sifting through that bullshit and start cleaning this joint up!

We've had a quick introduction to depression's lies, so far – from the simple confidence-bashing one-liners to the slightly more sophisticated lies that skew our perception of life events and leave us feeling paralysed. It's so important to challenge these lies because, if left to flourish, they prevent us from taking the steps that could help us feel better. For example, 'I am useless and fail at everything I try' will encourage us to give up on our recovery journey attempts, opting to carry on doing less. Similarly, if we're convinced we're too boring, we won't ever agree to seeing that friend who might remind us that we're not totally awful (or even brilliant!) to be around. Therefore, Rule 101 in dealing with depression's bullshit: we know its statements are lies (even if delivered in a shouty, authoritative voice) and it is our job to use our Low Mood Bullshit Translator to turn them into something more truthful – because, let's face it, we're fed up of depression getting in our way.

How do we replace the negativity with a more rational perspective? Where do we find the self-compassion to do that, when we may not have seen sight nor sound of it for months? Therapy initially helped me with this. I was taught that there is more than one way to interpret any situation, and that we can reframe our circumstances, depressed or not. We don't need a therapist to do this, we can develop our own voice of rationality – and close family members and friends can help us with this as a therapist would. That more positive, or neutral, voice might be small and quiet at first, but it's those first murmurings of truth that are so crucial.

Let's look at a couple of scenarios from opposing angles. Depressed or not, we can all imagine what we'd say to a friend who's feeling down.

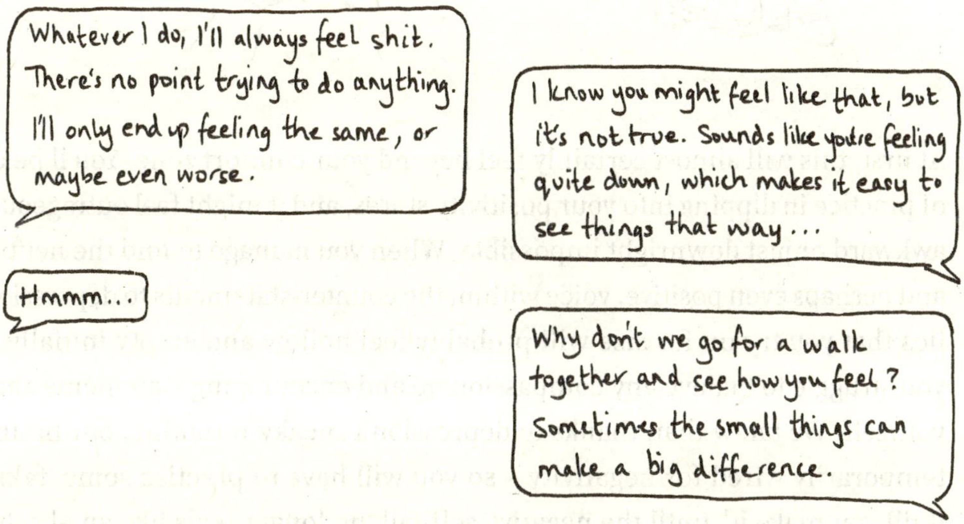

When we're helping our loved ones, we are easily able to draw on our stores of kindness, supportiveness and encouragement. A big part of being a good friend is to be their cheerleader, reminding them of how great they are when they can't find it in themselves. Our Low Mood Bullshit Translator is a little like being our own cheerleader (fewer pom-poms, though don't let me stop you).

At first, this will almost certainly feel beyond your comfort zone. You'll be out of practice in dipping into your positivity stores, and it might feel outrageously awkward or just downright impossible. When you manage to find the neutral, and perhaps even positive, voice within, the counter-statements to depression's lies that you try on for size will probably feel hollow and empty initially, as you struggle to believe any compassionate and encouraging statements about yourself. We know that, thanks to depression's sneaky rerouting, our brain is temporarily wired for negativity – so you will have to practise some 'faking it till you make it', until the negative self-talk no longer feels like an absolute truth. You don't need to suddenly believe it's all a big pile of lies, either. My first therapist would say that the most important change is from believing that a negative thought about yourself is 100% true to 99% true. Voila – we have the initial perception of doubt and, therefore, have challenged the assumption that our internal 'depression narrative' tells indisputable facts.

Often, it's not as easy as simply talking to ourselves like we would do a friend in need of a reassuring word. If it were that easy, I wouldn't have a whole book to write on pulling the rug from under depression. So, one thing I like to do, that makes it easier to remind myself that depression's lies are not facts, is use a 'distancing' technique. If I believe I'm useless, I say to myself, 'I have *noticed* that I am *having the feeling* that I am useless.' Here, I've called out the thought as exactly that – a thought or a 'feeling' – while taking a step back from it to 'notice' it. With that small amount of distance created, we can slide in a more realistic counter-statement.

* 'I'm not useless, I just didn't achieve very much today. But, actually, yesterday I did a lot more (and I can feel proud of that). Tomorrow is a new day.'
* 'I'm not on top form, but I'm probably not a *total* bore. I'll go to the party for a bit and see how I feel. Maybe it'll make me feel (even a tiny bit) better.'

Even gentle statements like these feel nice. We're treating ourselves with kindness and compassion – two things that depression really loathes. And if it's going to piss depression off, we want in!

Practising finding your voice of reason in the better times can be really effective. You could try an exercise my current therapist recommended: when you catch yourself hurling negativity at yourself, can you correct yourself with a more reasonable, maybe even positive, perspective? It may also help to have some useful comebacks to challenge depression, noted in your phone, ready for when you can't quite remember what a kickass human being you are. Friends and family are always better at seeing the good in us, so this is a great time to call on their help. Then, it's time to repeat and repeat and repeat those truths, until you're a bigger broken record than depression ever was!

Talk of gadgetry aside, I want to make it clear that no one needs a fancy trio of tools (not least an imaginary one that hasn't been, nor could ever be, invented) to do any of this. Really, we're just using the wonderfully unique ability that we all have to observe our thoughts from a different perspective. We're stepping out of the weeds to look at things with more clarity (something depression hates). While it may not be easy, it really is the cornerstone of how we can start to drown out depression's shouty negativity. As you practise it, and depression's slurs wear thin (and they likely will, as depression is often impatient and fickle), you'll be surprised at how often you might start to hear your own balanced voice of reason penetrating through the negative noise. It may feel pointless, you might even feel silly, repeating your counter-statements till you're blue in the face, but persistence really is your best friend here.

* * *

Self-monitoring and spotting the signs early are such brilliant skills to develop. Even so, we're not aiming to be self-monitoring super-bots, with inhuman powers, sniffing out low mood at a mind-boggling distance. Nor will we be fluent in translating depression's lies at first; it's much more likely that our voice of reason will start quietly and be unsure of itself. As with all parts of recovery, our aim is to look out for incremental gains, which eventually add up to a bigger, more beautiful picture – a work of art I like to call 'No One Cares about You and Your Lies, Depression.' A win might be noticing something about your depression that you didn't last time, spotting it just a tiny bit earlier, or asking a friend to keep an eye out for any signs. Any time you try to catch out depression's bullshit is something to be immensely proud of, and something you can build on.

* CHAPTER 12 *

There's No Such Thing as Failure

What if The Plan doesn't go to plan?

Tell me of a depression recovery journey that's gone entirely to plan, and I'd call you a fibber, then insist you write out 'The perfect recovery journey doesn't exist' a thousand times – because it doesn't.

We can quite easily think that an 'imperfect' recovery journey (i.e. one that doesn't go how we want or expected) makes us a failure, especially if this isn't our first dance with depression. My favourite unhelpful thought, as I come out of yet another supposedly 'sub-standard' recovery (by my own definition) is, 'You should be an expert at this by now, but you have failed, yet again.' This has been such a hard narrative to challenge. I've gradually managed it by working on knowing my worth and valuing the successes in my life, regardless of how I feel about myself in the moment. If anything, the fact that I'm no longer depressed is a huge achievement to feel deeply proud of. Equally, the times I stuck with it when depressed were also admirable. This narrative flip – from perceived failure to success – is crucial. It keeps my self-belief intact, when depression tries to decimate it, and it gives me that 'mental health confidence' that supports me on my onward journey.

We all need to remember: on any recovery journey (whether you're on one now or girding your loins for your next), there is No Such Thing as Failure. Good, I'm glad we got that sorted.

This is where the 'recovery squiggle' in Chapter 1 couldn't be truer. Sometimes we'll feel as if we're right back where we started; at others, it seems that we've taken a step or two or twenty thousand back. There were times that I wanted to crawl into a hole in the ground, after a 'disastrous' conversation with a friend, or days straight spent on the sofa. However, to label such wobbles as 'failure' means we're assessing ourselves or an event too harshly. One, ten or one hundred perceived 'hiccups' (and that's really what we should try to see them as) doesn't undo any of the progress we've made or invalidate our efforts up to now. There is not a single recovery journey that didn't make its owner feel as if they'd failed at some point.

So, it's decided – we're embracing this imperfect, squiggly recovery journey. All that zigging and zagging, falling and getting back up, can even be helpful. I hate to give depression credit for anything, but I'll hand it to the slimy pest – I have grown and learnt from it more than almost anything else in life.

Last year is the perfect example. I spent the whole year depressed. This was a truth I couldn't bring myself to acknowledge until I was better and had gone to therapy to address what had happened. I felt embarrassed that, for 95% of that year, The Plan didn't make it out of my metaphorical drawer – there was not even so much as a half-hearted flapping of paper from me. When I eventually started to introduce helpful activities and practise positive behaviours, these felt haphazard and unpredictable. My plan had certainly not gone to plan.

I could easily brand it my biggest recovery failure ever. Instead, I've done a lot of work to realize that I have grown in ways I only could through weathering that horrid inertia, making the unhelpful choices I sometimes made, and just getting through the self-hatred I felt. Lessons in self-compassion grew from those challenges and my thinking on low mood and depression has evolved drastically since. I've even added new chapters to this book as a result. What's more, as I notched up another dance with depression between starting and finishing writing, you're getting seven for the price of six in these pages! Silliness aside, the journey, while tough, has been essential. More than ever, my shame continues to shrink, and instead I often feel a pride that brings tears to my eyes when I think of all I've got through and grown from.

A bold statement though it may be, The Plan won't ever go exactly to plan. Mine never has and I don't suppose it ever will. We should, instead, feel supremely proud that we embarked on the journey to try and tell depression to 'just fuck off'. I know undoing a failure narrative takes more than reading a few paragraphs in a book, and I can't pick up your feelings of failure by the scruff of the neck and toss them out of the window while proclaiming, 'Be gone!' (though I would if I could). However, I hope that we can chip away at any misplaced assessments of ourselves, and you can start to feel proud of your twists and turns on this squiggly journey.

What if we're not where we want to be?

The majority of being depressed is spent feeling as if we aren't where we want to be, or where we 'should' be. In the laws of Depression Maths, take this feeling, add low self-esteem and self-loathing, multiply it by 'days spent depressed' and – ta da! – the sum of your equation equals FAILURE. Who can blame us? We live in a society that devalues anyone experiencing mental ill-health and wants us to believe that we could all feel okay in two weeks if we only popped those serotonin-filled pills. Paired with our own expectations, plus the very rational desire to simply feel 'a little less shit' (we're not even asking to feel great at this stage!), it's easy to see why we may judge ourselves for not being 'where we should be'.

I understand this feeling deeply. Six months into depression's last promenade through my life, I was fed up with having to bargain with myself to complete the smallest of tasks. Take my exhausting 'Great T-Shirt Change' campaign of depression visit #4 as an example, in which I had to pitch to myself the idea of changing the t-shirt I'd worn for three consecutive days. Even then I remained unconvinced; I was going to need a more compelling proposition to prize that crumpled khaki number off my unwashed back. I remember when doing the small things with ease and simply 'feeling okay again' was the stuff that dreams were made of. I understand the frustration of wanting to be anywhere else than where you are now.

When we first start making progress, that feeling doesn't disappear straightaway. This can be highly demotivating. Not one of us signed up for the Glacial Depression Recovery programme, whose brochure reads, 'Take your time meandering through depression's highs lows and lows. Immerse yourself in miserable, grey sights with a bunch of people who couldn't give a shit. Luxuriate in the total discomfort of it all while hating yourself. Why rush, when you can suffer slowly?'

If we've been depressed before, we know that no part of recovery is comfortable. However, while we may *want* to, and feel that we *should*, be somewhere else, I'm afraid to say that we're going to have to get comfortable with that discomfort. As hard as it may be, we need to get used to the idea that we will spend most of our time being precisely where we don't want to be. When we feel stuck, and even when we start to make progress, we may feel frustrated by the pace of change. However, here's the key reframe: that doesn't make us failures. Getting through depression is doing a whole load of shit we don't want to do – and that includes feeling things we'd much rather not. Accepting this feeling and sitting with it while we push through to the other side, as uncomfortable as that is, is one of those.

Sitting in a space of perceived failure (and I must stress that it is our *perception* of our situation, not reality) isn't easy, and here I am asking you to get comfortable in it. It may be the very definition of adding insult to injury. However, I have found that the times when I feel the greatest repulsion for the situation that I find myself in, and the discomfort it brings, are when I find myself finally taking the first step towards feeling better. That's not to say I would wish that feeling on anyone – if only I could give one and all the gift of a pleasant recovery journey! Sadly, I can't. However, pushing away from that place we don't want to be in really can give us our fire and keep us getting the hard shit done.

As I've said, it's not easy (enduring theme: depression ain't easy) and there will be so many times we want to throw our hands in the air and say, 'If you think this is so easy, you do it. I'm done!' So, there are a couple of things I'd like to share to make the process feel a little better. The first is self-compassion.

Finding that elusive self-compassion

As humans, being nice to ourselves seems to be monumentally difficult – and even more so when we're depressed and in need of it the most. That's because while depression is busy stripping all positivity from our life, it takes self-compassion right with it. If we can't see the positive in anything, it's very hard to find love, understanding and kindness to show ourselves. However, it isn't impossible and we can get good at practising our self-compassion when times are good, as well as bad. It's truly great for anyone's mental health, with the added bonus that depression despises it – so of course we want in.

Part of the reason we'll feel the pull to 'give up' on a recovery journey is the barrage of put-downs depression subjects us to. 'You're a piece of shit' seems to be my answer to everything in these moments, closely followed by, 'You're a failure.' Imagine if we could change that broken record to, 'That was a good first step; there's a way to go, but I think I'm getting there', or even, 'Never mind – let's try again tomorrow.' On a recovery journey that is never linear, these mini positive pep talks could be the difference between accepting the fate of the depression gods or pushing on (however tentatively). Self-compassion is the best kind of motivator, especially when we're not where we want to be. So, let's find a way to channel our love, kindness and empathy for the most deserving of people – ourselves!

Of course, while we're noticing the negative, remembering the negative and interpreting things negatively (remember our cognitive model from Chapter 2), we hardly have room for positive thoughts in that brain of ours, let alone the kind, loving, gentle self-talk that self-compassion requires. Recently, with the help of my therapist, I've come to believe that there is a way to tackle this.

In Chapter 4, I mentioned that I'm testing the theory, proposed by my therapist, that how we talk to ourselves when we're feeling good, or okay, could determine how we talk to ourselves when struggling. We're practising until the unnatural gradually feels that bit more natural. When we find ourselves down in the depression dumps, and we're unleashing our self-compassionate voice on depression – so that it comes up in a nasty, allergic rash – that voice is likely to be a little easier to find, less alien and more believable. As with any theory, the only way to test it is to give it a go, so perhaps you could try it out today.

What does self-compassion look like?

I know one thing self-compassion is not. It is not the toxic positivity meme-ified version we see on Instagram (e.g. 'I don't dwell on the negative. Think positive and everything will be okay!'). This over-saturated, over-simplified, heavily filtered incarnation is not realistic, nor is it what we're aiming for. We won't always be dripping in self-compassion, as social media might have us believe. It might come and go, or it might be quiet, almost imperceptible at times (especially when our mood is low). Self-compassion is also realistic and balanced, it acknowledges that things are hard and encourages us to be gentle with ourselves in the face of that.

It might start quietly, as we find our feet – in fact, this might be the best way to slip a bit of kind self-talk in unnoticed, while depression is too caught up in its own silly insults. A simple, 'It's okay, try again tomorrow' or, 'Just getting out for 15 minutes today was better than yesterday' could plant the seed for more kindness towards yourself. When my self-compassion shows up, it sounds more like this than grand statements about how I am deserving of love and kindness. Developing a quiet self-compassion is a wonderful goal to have and a fantastic starting point.

Some people practise self-compassion more naturally; they speak kindly to themselves and pick themselves up with gentle encouragement when things aren't going so well. This may sound like you, or, like many people who've had depression (including myself), we'll need to make a more concerted effort to embed these helpful practices into our daily life. My negative self-talk is fairly shouty and constant, so I'm thrilled if I can muster any kindness for myself, especially when down depression's dark, dank, dried-up well.

However yours looks (a whisper or singing it from the rooftops), the most important thing is that you learn to nurture it and develop your own self-compassionate voice. In our particular context, by 'self-compassion' I mean anything that challenges the barbed, negative thoughts about ourselves that depression disguises as our true beliefs.

Here are some examples of how we can dodge depression's nastiness and beat it at its own game.

Depression's negative voice	Gentle self-compassion	Singing it from the rooftops self-compassion
You can't even get out of bed; you're a lazy, good-for-nothing waste of space (and your bed linen needs washing, ya filthy animal).	I am disappointed that I haven't got out of bed yet, but I'll get out of bed a bit later. There's nothing wrong with rest and if I was feeling better then I might get up (p.s. washing my bed linen isn't a priority when I'm so low in energy).	You try getting out of bed when you feel like everything in the world is pointless! This is all I can manage right now, so I'll stay in bed until I can manage more. Rest can be positive and productive. As for the bedding, I don't care, to be honest. I've got bigger fish to fry.
Don't bother going out tonight. Your friends don't like you; they think you're a waste of space and awful to be around, and they're right. You'd be better off staying in that smelly cave you call a bedroom and ignoring everyone's texts.	I know that going out tonight to see my friends is probably the best thing for me. I feel as if my friends don't like me, but I think I'm a good person and they probably do care about me. I just can't see it right now. I don't think I can bring myself to go out tonight but that's okay. I'll text them and say I'm sorry and that I'd like to try another day. They'll understand.	I recognize this old, boring 'You're shit to be around' soundtrack loop. I feel as if I'm a piece of shit to be around, but I must remember that I'm not. I'm caring, loving and thoughtful, and my friends value me for all these qualities and more. I just can't see it so easily tonight, so I'll text my friends to explain. Screw you depression – *you're* a smelly cave.
You're totally unloveable. Your parents, siblings, partner, friends (and everyone else you know) don't love you. Why would they? I can't see a single thing that there is to love about you.	I may not be able to see the things that are loveable about me right now, but I think there probably are some. It's okay if I can't see them. My family, partner and friends loved me before so it's likely that they still love me now.	Oh my gosh, I am loveable. I don't feel it but I can remember all the times my friends, family and partner have told me how much they love me. I can still see it in the way they show up for me, even now. I can't expect to feel that I'm worthy of love right now but that doesn't mean I'm not.

cont.

Depression's negative voice	Gentle self-compassion	Singing it from the rooftops self-compassion
You're a total failure. You'll never amount to anything.	I feel like a failure right now but there is some evidence that I haven't failed at everything in life until this point. This might not be my finest hour and I may not be where I want to be, but this probably isn't failure. I'm doing what I feel I can at the moment – that's enough for now.	Mate, have you looked at yourself? I'd say that going around making people's lives a misery is the real failure in this situation. Know what I did today? I got out of bed, brushed my teeth, made myself breakfast *and* ate it. For someone with depression, that's success. I've succeeded at tons before and this tricky patch doesn't make me a failure. For now, showing up and taking on life is the biggest achievement there is.

You'll notice some recurring phrases and similar sentiments in the above:

* '...and that's okay.'
* 'I might be feeling like this now but...'
* 'I know I feel like... But actually...'
* 'I may not be able to see that... But...'

I have one more important addition: 'Fuck you, depression' (used to best effect when at the end of our tether). I find that this one can be especially effective.

We're challenging the idea that a) we have always felt/been like this, and b) we will always feel/be like this. The first step is to remind ourselves that we only feel this way *now*; we could feel differently tomorrow, next week or at any point. Next, we counter it with a 'but...' and remind ourselves that we have felt and behaved differently in the past: 'But...I used to feel so loved by my friends. I'd have so much fun on a night out.' And maybe, just maybe, we are still all those wonderful things – all we need is that seed of doubt (taking our belief that we're awful from 100% to 99%). I'll let you in on a secret: we most definitely are still as wonderful but we just can't see that right now. Lastly, 'It's okay' is a small but powerful statement. We may not be our favourite version of ourselves, and perhaps we're operating at 20% rather than 100%, but that's okay! We're allowed dips and it won't be this way forever.

I hope the ways depression likes to talk to us, and how we can respond, may be familiar to you by now. Think back to our Low Mood Bullshit Detector (in Chapter 11); you'll recognize that Depression Voice because, as we now know, depression's lies and insults are limited and predictable, but annoyingly convincing. The self-compassionate voice we're developing in response is our way to drown out that noise. Once we've sniffed out the bullshit with our Low Mood Bullshit Detector, we can remind ourselves of how we used to feel about ourselves and who we still are.

This stuff isn't easy (no surprises there). We may be unlearning coping strategies we've perfected from a young age – to push ourselves, to avoid disappointment, or because we believe unhelpful comments made to us in childhood. Traditionally, I have encouraged and listened to that nasty voice in my head – it's felt like a helpful tool to try harder, be better, and achieve more, using 'success' to prove it wrong and avoid the pain of 'failure'. That doesn't mean a negative internal driver (as many of us have) is good for us if we don't use it in moderation. Rather, we've become adept at using it in specific contexts. As you try to upgrade this strategy to a self-compassionate one, focus on being kind and patient with yourself, just as you would with anyone learning something new.

Outsourcing our self-compassion

A great way to model our self-talk is to imagine how we talk to a good friend. We speak with kindness, love and support and we tell them how great they are. The thing is, when we're struggling, we simply don't have this in us. What do you expect? We've been doing the Depression-lympics for months on end (less pole-vaulting, more 'sofa-sitting', for which I am the proud owner of a gold medal), so we need to work on these skills. Hopefully we can start practising, using the tips I've shared. In the meantime, we can outsource some of our self-compassion needs!

Let me take you back to the time I got a kind, supportive text from my friend (in Chapter 1). I believed her when she told me that I'd seemed brighter and chattier. While depression still tried to convince me that I had the personality of a cement mixer, my friend had 'lent' me her kindness and positivity, so I could see that depression was probably wrong about me. Her compassion had planted a kernel that my own self-compassion could sprout from and my job was to continue to water it when I could.

We are aiming to build our own self-compassion muscles that we can flex as soon as we hear the dismal drone of depression. In the meantime, it is more than okay to lean on our loved ones for that buoyant voice we can't yet muster ourselves. I'd encourage you to be as deliberate and proactive about it as you can. Try having a conversation with a couple of trusted people in your support crew, telling them that your inner critic is currently very shouty, and that it really helps to hear nice things about yourself (even if you don't believe them right now) – would they mind sharing a few nice words from time to time? No need to tell this Brit how cringey that might feel. But, of all the difficulties we'll face when digging ourselves out of a depression hole, asking a mate to say, 'Actually, you're a great person', is one of the more pleasant 'awkward' things we'll need to do!

* * *

I believe that with every attempt at talking to ourselves as if we're someone who is worth loving – or even just liking, if that's all we can manage – we are exercising our self-compassion muscles. As with progress in the gym, with every 'workout' (trying to drown out depression's bullshit with some self-compassion) we get 'stronger' (more resilient, and better at being kind to ourselves, regardless of the circumstances). Just like building muscle, it takes time and consistency, but putting in effort always gives results.

So, try working on that self-compassionate voice that really is somewhere inside you still. When you're feeling good, get practising, and try being ludicrously lovely to yourself; perhaps it'll come more naturally next time life gets tough. And remember, while we're working on our Incredible Hulk-like compassion muscles, you can always ask a mate for a compliment to spur you on!

The Plan was made to be rewritten

Our self-compassion is crucial in accepting our situation, wherever we find ourselves. When used, we're less likely to throw ourselves into a vortex of self-admonishment, which could send us whooshing even further down depression's slimy garbage chute. It helps us accept that The Plan won't always go to plan and to feel okay with that. Remember, The Plan never (or rarely) does go to plan, so let's make that part of our Plan right now (aka the 'depression double bluff').

One of my favourite quotes is, 'We can't control what happens to us, but we can control how we react to it.' Our first plan not quite hitting the mark may be out of our hands, but asking ourselves, 'So now what?' and finding a way forward, is ours for the taking. It may take a simple tweaking of The Plan – a nip and a tuck – to try a slightly different tact. Or you may want to pull your Plan apart and stick it back together in a drastically different form. Either way, change (however small) is what is called for if we're not taking steps forward in the direction we'd like.

As with any strategizing or planning that we do around our mental health, doing it with someone else (a therapist or one of our support crew) is always helpful, holds us to account and, crucially, feels far less burdensome. Plus, trying to push ourselves outside our Depression Comfort Zone in a new way can feel scary or daunting, so lean on the comfort of your crew if you can.

Whether you have the help of someone else, or you're going solo, here's my revision cheat sheet. It will help you consider what changes you could make, when and why, as you give your Plan a glow-up.

THE REVISION CHEAT SHEET

Why might it be time for a change?

You may feel like it's time to shake things up if you're not seeing the progress you'd like, or expected, or any progress at all. You may feel stuck because you're not pushing yourself outside your Depression Comfort Zone, to make depression nice and uneasy, or your goals are so far outside that comfort zone that you've overwhelmed yourself into running back into your depression cave.

What kind of change is needed?

You either need to tweak your Plan so you're pushing yourself more in the activities you schedule, so you feel more challenged but still not pushed unreasonably hard. Or you need to dial things back, so that those activities feel more manageable, and you can begin to take steps forward (rather than doing your favourite cave scuttle).

What changes to your activities can you make?

* **Adjust the frequency:** If you'd aimed to do something social once a week and you're finding that you're bored and twiddling your thumbs, try socializing twice a week or more – even, and especially, if it feels a little uncomfortable. The best way is to make plans with people and put them in your diary in advance rather than being more fluid. On the flip side, if three gym sessions a week haven't been achievable, and that makes you feel as if you're failing, try a weekly session. If you're already at the minimum you can do to make sure you've got your essential Plan Pie slices perfectly baked (e.g. you've just about got your connection, purpose and support crew slices filled), my advice is to keep those in because you can make other adjustments...
* **Adjust the intensity:** Is that one social plan a week you'd promised yourself not materializing? It's a good idea to look at how much that planned activity demands of you. If you're trying to join a group of mates on a big night out, starting off with a few drinks and 'seeing where the night takes us', you'll probably be so far out of your Depression Comfort Zone that depression is going to start kicking up an almighty fuss. I wouldn't blame you for never making it out. Instead, try planning some 'quiet socializing' with one or two friends you feel comfortable with. Perhaps visit a chilled cafe during the day or go on a dog walk in the park. If that's the kind of socializing you've already aced, and you're after the next step, you could try joining in with a group and pushing yourself that bit closer to the types of things you used to do with friends. The same could be done with your exercise routine. If going to the gym has felt like an insurmountable task, perhaps just commit to 15 minutes on the cross trainer at a time when the gym is quieter. If that feels easy, maybe it's time for the challenge of that buzzy interval training class you used to love.

What if communicating your needs feels awkward?

It can be tricky to express our needs and sometimes we might feel as if we're letting friends down (e.g. if we're not up for their big birthday bash). It's a great idea to have some stock phrases ready that you can use to communicate effectively and with less stress.

With my therapist's help, I learnt to say to friends, 'I'm sorry, I'm feeling really low/not so great at the moment and don't feel up to a group meetup. Would you mind if you and I met in a cafe during the day, or found a cosy pub?' Or it might be, 'I'm sorry I can't come to the pub on Friday. I've been struggling lately so I'm planning my socializing carefully to not feel overwhelmed. Would you mind if we met next week instead?'

Of course, the response was nothing other than enthusiastic support. Most friends just want to see you, however works best for you (probably with a dose of sweet relief; so many people I know would jump at the chance to be in bed by 10pm!).

* **Switch up the activities:** Maybe whatever you've picked for your initial plan doesn't float your boat as you expected. It's likely that you've had a long 'fallow' period while feeling low, so your capacity may be different or your tastes might have changed, as you adjust to gradually 'coming back to life'. A change is as good as a rest, so have a go at a completely new hobby (I took up football during my last recovery and it's now one of my greatest loves) or try something else you used to enjoy but didn't put on your Plan originally. You might like to put a different spin on something you used to enjoy; for example, Good Gym combines fitness activities with social causes. You could run to deliver an elderly person their shopping, which might be the motivation you need to kick-start your fitness routine (find their details on my website; my weblink is given at the end of the book). You could see this as a unique chance to experiment with new things that work for you.

What result are you hoping for?

My current therapist taught me the power of taking control of the things that are within our power to control. We can't get depression to disappear just because we said so (chance would be a fine thing!), but we can show it that we're not at its mercy and we won't be falling at the first hurdle. Revising The Plan says, 'I call the shots, not you, depression.' This, in itself, is a huge win.

In terms of outcomes, you'd hope to see a little more progress in the areas you've revised and tweaked. They probably won't be great big leaps and bounds just yet (though they could be!) However, small tweaks are likely to yield incremental change. But we've been learning to notice those steps, both small and large, and we can use that to motivate and propel us forward on our onward journey (and shove depression in a burning bin).

What next?

Keep a beady eye on things! These are some tips we can use to guide how we turn The Plan into something that truly works for us. You are the keeper of your Plan, its future and your progress from here. It might be that your first revision hits the spot, or that you revise things a couple of times, especially as you progress along your recovery journey and need to find new ways to stay outside that Depression Comfort Zone. By regularly self-monitoring (with the help of your trusty Self-Monitoring Majig from Chapter 10) and assessing how you're doing – with a therapist or one of your support crew, if possible – you're likely to make sure your Plan is effective, suited to you, and that you see the incremental progress you're hoping for.

I'd love you to use my cheat sheet to guide the revisions you make to your Plan, if and when they are needed. More than anything, I'd like you to cling tightly to the concept that underpins these tips. Revising The Plan is part of The Plan – it always was, all along. The Plan was made to be rewritten. You haven't failed – far from it.

* CHAPTER 13 *

The Maintenance Plan

Finding sustainability: The 'maintenance plan'

What I feared most after realizing just how disgusting depression feels was the thing making an appearance again. While I've learnt that our value is not measured by how many times we do or don't get depressed, the thought of something that brings so much pain and disruption turning up again is a very real nightmare that I'd rather not revisit. None of us is very keen on it making a return, to say the very least.

Therefore, it makes sense that we'll be looking for a way to stay on an even keel, in good and less good times. I call my approach to staying on that even plane my 'maintenance plan' – it's a 'belts and braces' bolt-on to The Plan, to make sure I'm doing all I can to look after myself and my mental health, when I'm no longer languishing in a hole and would like it to stay that way. I would urge anyone who has been in the depression doldrums to invest in a maintenance plan for the peace of mind it can bring.

Here are the main components of mine:

* therapy with a trusted therapist (when I feel it is beneficial)
* an exercise routine/movement
* socializing in a way that feels good and manageable (it's just as important that I don't overdo it)
* scheduling evenings that I keep free (otherwise I have a habit of forgetting to rest)

* going into the office for work regularly
* cooking and eating balanced, tasty meals
* journalling every morning, when I can.

These are on my maintenance plan because I know that they have all helped me out of a sticky situation and continue to be good for me once depression has run for the hills. Yours might be similar or completely different. Below are some more examples of habits we might find on a maintenance plan. They don't have to be grand achievements, or even targeted mental health 'treatments'; they're simply things we know help us feel better (often called acts of 'self-care'):

* sufficient rest
* time alone to recharge your batteries
* drinking alcohol only in moderation or avoiding it completely
* a meditation/mindfulness practice
* going for a daily walk
* dancing to banging tunes every morning
* reciting positive affirmations.

This list isn't exhaustive. Anything that keeps us engaging in life in a healthy way, and keeps us further away from a dip in mood, is a brilliant candidate for our maintenance plan.

Just as only we can lead in our recovery, so too is it down to us to take care of our ongoing well-being – I believe this means making sure we have a maintenance plan in place. Thankfully, we all have the ability to do this and to look after our own mental health. I quickly realized that if I was going to get good at this game, no one could do it for me. While others can support me, I need to be the one that is in tune with myself and how my actions and behaviour affect my mood. That is why I believe there are two essential skills we need to practise, to pull off a shit hot maintenance plan:

1. **Self-awareness:** To make a plan that keeps things ticking along nicely once we've given depression the heave-ho, we ideally need to know ourselves and what was going on when depression set up camp. By revisiting the possible causes, we can find ways to live our lives that avoid certain behaviours or unhelpful coping mechanisms, or we can fill our lives with things that counter the root cause (e.g. if loneliness contributed to our depression, how can we find ways to fill it with human connection?).

2. **Self-monitoring:** We're all familiar with my Self-Monitoring Majig by now (from Chapter 10). It is our way of keeping a beady eye on the day-to-day, how things might be shifting and changing, how we're feeling and if The Plan might need revising. Thankfully, as we're in training to be self-monitoring masters, we have an idea of how to spot warning signs and engage with any plan we have prepared accordingly – whether that be the maintenance plan, once our mood has lifted, or The Plan we kick into action in the face of a pesky onslaught from depression.

* * *

There is more to the maintenance plan than keeping our mental health from teering on the edge of a mental health hole we'd rather not visit. I want you to have a maintenance plan for the peace of mind and confidence it can bring – a feeling of greater control after the weeks, months and years when depression likely stole that from you. As the choppy waters are gradually calmed to stillness, it is easy to feel rudderless; we're left to navigate the life we've suddenly picked back up. The memory of that storm will never disappear, so a plan for 'What now?' can give us direction and help us feel safe.

Making our maintenance plan

I like to think of the maintenance plan as the more joyous part of this whole business. We can think of it as an extension of The Plan (the one we used to whip depression into shape in the first place). Pleasingly, this one shouldn't make our skin crawl at the thought of following it, as we'll no longer be stuck in

Depression's Comfort Zone. We'll be taking those familiar Plan Pie slices (from Chapter 5) and making sure we're tucking into them in a new way – we can up the intensity, pleasure and enjoyment of activities we were doing, or keep them the same if they feel right. The maintenance plan can be the fulfilling, enjoyable part of this whole business, as we make sure we're living the full life we deserve – one with moments of joy – while developing a stability that helps us ride out some of life's inevitable tougher moments.

To remind ourselves, the slices that I included in my Plan Pie were:

* socializing and connection
* support system
* activities and hobbies
* exercise, diet, sleep (lifestyle)
* purpose
* work.

It's up to you to decide on your pie slices and how large each is – for example, if exercise is a non-negotiable in your daily routine, it might take up a large portion of your maintenance Plan Pie. An equally pivotal factor is that our Plan is responsive and reactive. We can moderate the scale, volume, pace and intensity of our activities based on how manageable it feels, or our needs, at any time. This goes for when we're coming out of a depression dip, and finding our feet, just as much as when depression feels like a distant memory and we're navigating the normal ups and downs of life. Our self-awareness helps us determine our personal thresholds, and self-monitoring helps us realize when we're coming close to, or pushing past, them.

A maintenance plan can feel especially important when we've only just raised ourselves out of the depression quagmire. I want to explore how we can plan our activities in a way that is sensitive to the fact that we may be feeling a little fragile, but with an eye on operating as our fullest selves eventually. Here is an example of how our maintenance plan might evolve.

Activity	Weeks after depression/Frequency of activities	
	1–6	7+
Gym	Once weekly	3–4 times weekly
Seeing friends	Once weekly	2–3 times weekly
Hobbies	None right now	Once a week at first (perhaps working up to two if it brings you enjoyment)
Going to the office	Twice weekly	2–4 times weekly

A depression dance really does take it out of you (it's the most chaotic, unpredictable dance around), so it's best to have a plan that starts at a comfortable pace, but outside your old Depression Comfort Zone (weeks 1–6 above), and gradually builds you up to full capacity (weeks 7+ above). The timelines are yours to define – you might be upgrading your activity levels after months, rather than weeks.

The focus here is on adaptability and, most importantly, sustainability. Think of it as a maintenance manual of sorts, a guide that we keep by our sides and refer to from now until eternity – it's that useful. As new versions of ourselves and our life are 'released' or we get an 'upgrade', we issue a new user manual in the form of the maintenance plan, and that's all part of it. It is our investment in a sustainable, balanced life, whatever that looks like for you. It might be how things were before depression descended, or it might be a little different, if that's better right now – there is no template.

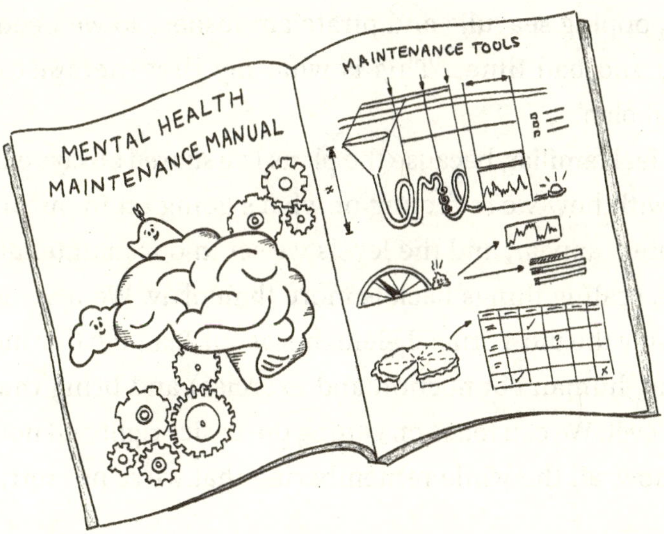

As always, there is a role for our support crew in this. Our truest cheerleaders are not only there for when things feel at their hardest or worst; they're one of our greatest levellers in a world that can feel rocky at times. They're part of our Plan Ecosystem (from Chapter 4), and help to keep us flourishing through the storms, droughts and beautifully bright days. A maintenance plan is something to be proud of, and your support crew are sure to feel delighted to play whatever role they can in yours.

* * *

I've come to understand that learning to live with depression is so much about learning to love and trust ourselves. This applies through the depression itself (when we can muster it), but especially 'out the other side', when we have the opportunity to build the confidence and sense of safety that we all deserve. The maintenance plan can be a hugely powerful part of this. It has helped me develop a feeling of agency, trust and control in my onward journey that I thought I may never have. I have no doubt that it can do the same for you too.

Life isn't always plain sailing: Our bi-directional plan

Our Good Ship Mental Health is never guaranteed to sail only the smoothest of seas – we know life isn't like that. Sometimes my boat is more like a dinghy being pummelled by the waves than a smooth and steady vessel. There'll be sea storms, pooping seagulls and pirate ambushes, so we need to be ready for the good and bad times. This is what my first therapist would call a 'bi-directional plan'.

This may feel familiar, because the plans I've shared always exist in phases, and morph with how we're feeling or what's going on in our life. So, when turbulent waters appear, and the levels we set in our maintenance plan feel unattainable, scaling things back is more than okay. We may need to really home in on only the most crucial elements of our Plan Pie (for me, that would be socializing, human connection and exercise) and bring those back to a manageable level. We can focus on getting the basics right and not worry about the rest for now, all the while remembering that we're not retreating to our

Depression Comfort Zone, but rather, doing a little jig just outside it (and, boy, does that piss depression off).

There may also be the opposite end of the experience to consider. Like me, you might be prone to some 'life highs' as well as the lows. There are times when I want to say yes to every opportunity that comes my way and cram so much into my time that overwhelm is a very real possibility. Here, we would use our maintenance plan to regulate our activity, putting thresholds in place to scale things back, for slightly different reasons compared to when we're feeling too stretched by life, but with the same goal – sustainability.

It's not always easy to notice these shifts or to make the changes we need. I feel so darn capable when I feel good that it can be hard to gauge that I'm overstretching myself, which can eventually be just as detrimental as shutting myself off from the world.

For this reason, we have yet another job for our support crew on our hands (I told you that they're useful!). My best friends, and often my therapist, have always been the best feedback if they've thought I'm going too hard at life, or seeming a little quiet and withdrawn. Try to keep an open dialogue with the people you love and trust. They can be uncomfortable conversations, with truths we sometimes don't want to hear ('What do you mean I shouldn't be busy every second of every day – I feel fantastic! You just don't get it.') but they can be the best support in helping us stick to a balanced maintenance plan.

Sustainability is our North Star that we are forever aiming for. To do this, we need to make sure we are ready for good and bad times, operating within the bounds that will keep us ticking along nicely. Your maintenance plan is here to help you, and I know – with an inevitable bit of trial and error (it really is key in this journey) – you can settle on one that feels like the right plan at the right time for you.

Mental health is like flossing

I know I run the risk of alienating about 90% of you, who find establishing a regular flossing routine a next to impossible task. I'm right there with you. However, bear with me and this comparison, because it works.

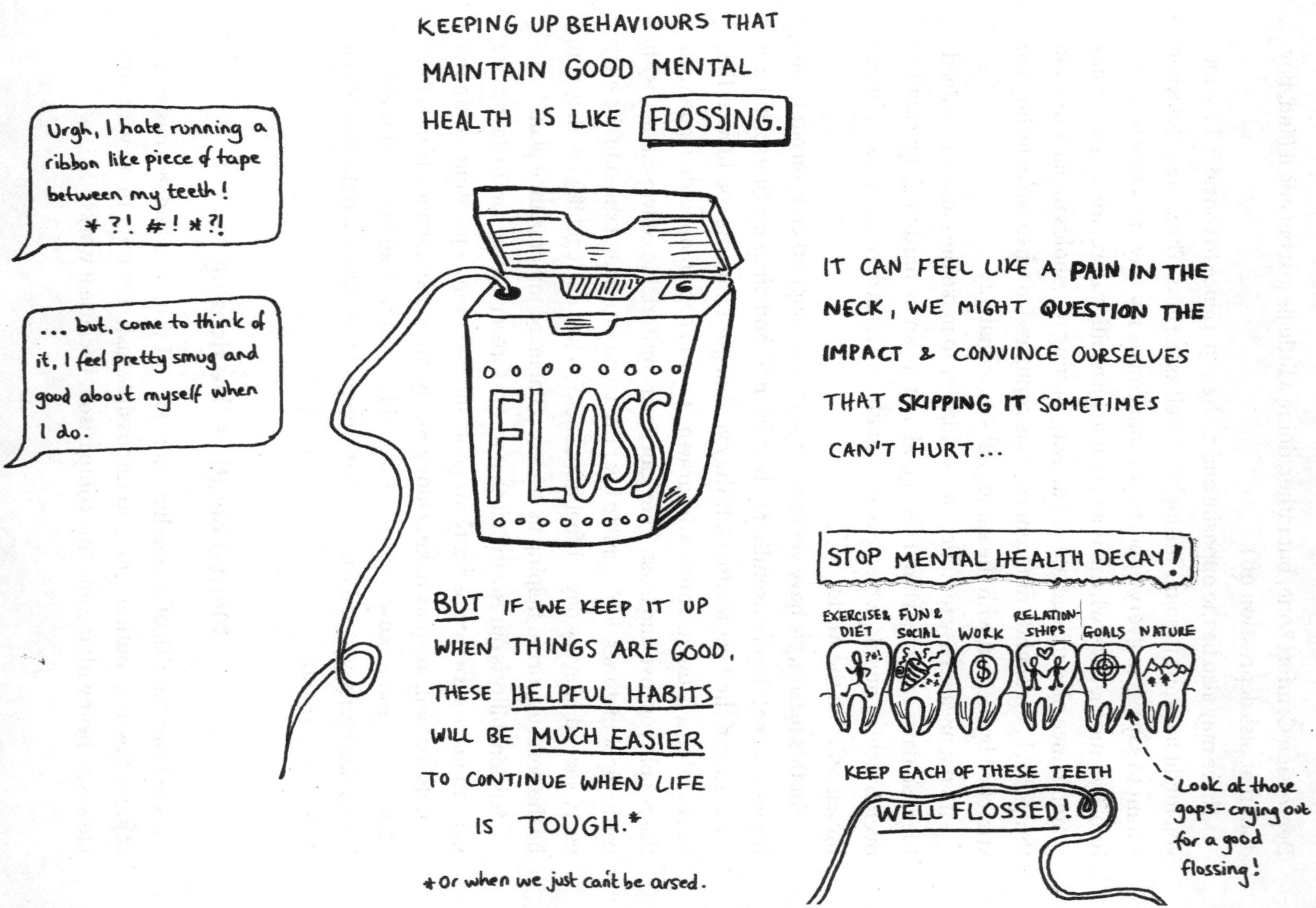
KEEPING UP BEHAVIOURS THAT MAINTAIN GOOD MENTAL HEALTH IS LIKE FLOSSING.
Urgh, I hate running a ribbon like piece of tape between my teeth! *?! #! *?!
... but, come to think of it, I feel pretty smug and good about myself when I do.
FLOSS
BUT IF WE KEEP IT UP WHEN THINGS ARE GOOD, THESE HELPFUL HABITS WILL BE MUCH EASIER TO CONTINUE WHEN LIFE IS TOUGH.*
*Or when we just can't be arsed.
IT CAN FEEL LIKE A PAIN IN THE NECK, WE MIGHT QUESTION THE IMPACT & CONVINCE OURSELVES THAT SKIPPING IT SOMETIMES CAN'T HURT...
STOP MENTAL HEALTH DECAY!
EXERCISE & DIET
FUN & SOCIAL
WORK
RELATIONSHIPS
GOALS
NATURE
KEEP EACH OF THESE TEETH WELL FLOSSED!
Look at those gaps – crying out for a good flossing!

Flossing is good for us (whether we like to admit it or not), but we don't always feel like doing it. It's boring, doesn't feel like a high priority, it's hard to see the benefits, and can feel rather pointless, especially when we're tired and ready for bed. If I tell a white lie, *surely* the dentist won't know? Answer: they *always* know.

Here's where I get to prove that flossing is just like our mental health maintenance plan. However we feel about flossing, it is *always* good for our teeth. The benefits will be felt most acutely when we incorporate it into our daily routine. We should do it, even when we don't feel like it, for the sake of our gum health. Looking after our mental health, with a maintenance plan, is no different. We must continue to keep up the behaviours, habits and routines we put in action when we weren't in a great place even when we're in a better place, to help stay on an even keel.

That's because, if we practise in the good times, these behaviours and habits won't feel quite so impossible when our heads are in, or inching closer to, the depression gutter. If we keep practising, until these helpful actions feel like a pair of well-worn slippers – so comfy, we barely notice them – we're less likely to respond, 'What the bleeding hell do you mean, I need to go for a long walk every day, make healthy meals *and* socialize?!' Of course, it will still feel hard (what part of depression doesn't?), but it shouldn't feel totally alien. We'll be working our way back to a familiar equilibrium, rather than an unrecognizable version of ourselves.

There will be times when our flossing, or our maintenance plan, starts to slip a little. There have been days when I look around and realize my plan is scrumpled up and gathering dust down the side of the sofa. That's okay – we can dust it off and set ourselves back on the right path again, with some refocusing. Our commitment to flossing in the long term is what counts; the odd lapse is inevitable in life's hecticness. It's all part of our learning journey, so if this feels like you too, don't worry – you're on the right path.

Think of me as your depression dentist, urging you to get that mental health floss out. I hope you now have an idea of the healthy habits and activities you should try to do routinely, so you feel good – they form your maintenance plan. We need those habits and routines strung along a reel of minty fresh tape, and gliding through your life, in and around each of your days, just like teeth, with all the predictability of someone who has impeccable dental hygiene. Good days, bad days, every day. We can all get good at flossing.

* CHAPTER 14 *

The Aftermath

Nurturing our mental health confidence

In the past, the very fact that I had been depressed, or might be depressed again, was enough to leave my confidence shrivelled into nothingness. My belief was that I was an awful human being, at fault for my own depression – cue feelings of guilt and shame. Even when things were good, I believed I was tentatively clinging onto life until the next time that depression inevitably razed everything to the ground again. These feelings often linger even once depression has skedaddled, as we're left to navigate it all in 'The Aftermath' – what I call the bit after depression. There is nothing in my life that has felt more complicated.

In the game of Depression Top Trumps (the worst card game on the market), one of depression's top skills is 'confidence crushing'. It never misses a chance to leave your confidence that bit more tattered than before it turned up. Sometimes it'll be completely steamrolled to the ground; other times, it may be left a little bruised and in need of a bit of care and attention. It's likely to depend on the flavour of your depression – how long it's stuck around for and how resilient and confident you were feeling before it came and did its worst. Whatever the scale, I've never met anyone whose confidence didn't take a hit during or after depression.

Over my various dealings with low mood, I developed a little confidence, hoping that with each depression dance (tango, waltz, cha cha cha, bachata, west coast swing, jive and Lindy Hop – the full seven I've learnt so far), that confidence would increase. Sometimes, and in some ways – as I invested in understanding this most confusing of 'things' – it did. That is, until my depression Lindy Hop last year (less of a 'hop', more of a crawl), when depression stole it all away once more. I couldn't admit to myself, or anyone else, that I'd been depressed – in my eyes, I'd just been criminally shit for a year (ALERT! LOW MOOD'S BULLSHIT!). I had to do a lot of work in and out of therapy to rewrite that narrative, rediscover my self-belief and remind myself that none of this was my fault. Our confidence – mental health-related, or otherwise – waxes and wanes, which can be trying. However, we can work on laying some sturdier foundations.

What is mental health confidence?

'Mental health confidence' is always personal to the individual. So much so that I've realized that I can only hope to convey what it means to me, so we can start to explore this together.

My mental health confidence does not come from the belief that depression will never darken my door again. I used to cling on to the hope that it wouldn't, to feel safe and secure, but I have chosen to no longer hang everything on that belief. I was leaning on it because I felt I couldn't deal with going through 'it' all again. Instead, I find more resolve and self-confidence in saying, 'I'd rather not do it again, but if I do, I will get through it – just like every other time.' I've tried to remove any self-judgement in the process. While I hope that the next go will be nothing more than a brief tickle of depression, I've vowed to stop putting pressure on myself to deal with it faster or to know exactly what I'm doing. Instead of these unimportant measures, my confidence comes in other guises.

Knowing I have prepared

This means preparing for depression as best I can, with the tools and knowledge I have available to me at the time. The emphasis is on doing what I feel able to and removing the weight of unrealistic expectations or a perfection that doesn't exist. You'll be familiar with the ways in which I prepare – it's everything I've shared so far. For example, I'll have worked with a therapist and implemented those learnings as best I can; I'll have engaged my support crew as much as I feel able to; and I'll have practised my self-compassion when things have felt lighter. This preparation gives me confidence because I know that these things will help me give depression a savage clip round the ear when we next cross paths. Just as importantly, I can also feel proud of how I set out to look after my mental health to the best of my ability.

Knowing that I will get through it

I don't know how I'll get through my next depression dance, if I have one. All I know is that I *will* get through it – and so will you. Even with all the lessons I've learnt through therapy and living the damn thing, we can't always stop depression swooping in and getting its mess everywhere, like a chorus of unruly seagulls, pooping all over the deck of our Good Ship Mental Health. That's okay, I didn't summon them there (for a start, I don't speak seagull) and I've no reason to feel like a failure because they turned up. I know that I will kick, shove, muddle and drag myself through that depression-y mess, cleaning as I go, until I can one day hopefully stand with a feeling of peace on a clearer ship deck. We may get back to where we once were, if that's the goal, or we may end up somewhere a little different (both are valid). Either way, my confidence comes from knowing that I have, I can and I will make it through depression, in the only way I know how – and that I should feel immensely proud of myself for that.

Knowing that I can turn to my support crew – and that I deserve their support

We can't always rely on our own skills in the midst of a depression whirlwind. That thing blows in and leaves us twisted upside down and unable to tell right from left. Thankfully, I know one group of incredible humans who will stand strong: my support crew, who will do what they can should I be left feeling a little (or very) helpless. The sense of safety, security and support that this group of people provide me with means that I know I don't have to go through this alone. I can feel more confident knowing that they've got my back.

We know depression lies, because it'll do anything to keep us where we are; Instead, let's listen to the people who love and care about us. If they tell you that you can do it, I urge you to believe them and lean into the belief they have in you. And, for what it's worth, I believe wholeheartedly in you, too.

* * *

I haven't tried to pretend that I have an innate, unstoppable confidence in how I manage my mood. It's important to me that I show you that building mental health confidence is always a work in progress; no one has this all figured out. Some days, I don't have any confidence that I could put half my advice into practice. With time, I'm gradually developing my self-belief, and building an understanding of my depression and how best to approach it, and that does bolster the trust I have in myself. While that grows slowly – and often with a wobbly uncertainty – my confidence comes from knowing that I'm doing my best, I'm learning and I have people around me who care. No one has a perfectly elegant dance with depression, whether it be their first or their fiftieth – mine have all been sluggish, sometimes chaotic, always lacking in rhythm and downright exhausting. But I know that, no matter how things have looked, I have a 100% success record of making it to the end of that dismal dance and surviving (even when I've not wanted to). That amazing feat alone is reason enough for any of us to feel proud and confident in ourselves.

There's a favourite quote of mine, by the author Haruki Murakami, that sums it up well:

> Once this storm is over you won't remember how you made it through, how you managed to survive. You won't even be sure, in fact, whether the storm is really over. But one thing is certain. When you come out of the storm you won't be the same person who walked in. That's what this storm's all about.[8]

My life does not look the same now as it did before the first time that I experienced depression, 12 years ago. Nor does my confidence. That's because I've made it through that storm, and I am no longer the same person. In some ways, I feel more uncertain. I no longer have a peaceful (and perhaps naive) trust in life being smooth and stable. But in navigating my own choppy mental health seas, to have nurtured the resilience I have been able to, and to have steered myself home to 'me' every time depression has thrown my boat off course – that is a new confidence, a different confidence, and one that I could never have expected for myself.

I don't believe depression is sent to teach us anything. I don't believe there is inherent meaning in it. But that there can be movement and growth alongside it, even when we feel that it has stripped us of everything worthwhile, makes this whole thing a little less pointless – and even meaningful.

Feeling bad about feeling bad

For a moment, let's pretend that we've internalized, without questioning, all of society's messages about mental health, mood and our feelings (gosh, poor us). We'd probably believe that most people feel okay in themselves most of the time and that to experience any 'mental health issue' is a deviation from the 'norm' (if such a thing existed). It's easy to see why, in this context, whenever we felt shit, we'd feel apprehensive to share openly about it. How odd for something that sits on a very typical spectrum of human feelings, I always think.

Since I've got to know depression, I have picked up all sorts of friends along this unpredictable and bumpy journey. Many of them I wouldn't have met if it hadn't been for my 'imperfect' mental health: friends I met at a mental health charity, when I was too depressed to work, or at mental health events, or even at football, the sport I started to try and very literally kick my low mood into oblivion. The beauty of picking up friends along the way is that they know me as the version of myself I am today – that person is bolder in how she talks about her mental health experiences. By sharing, I've found out that all these friends have been through a period of 'imperfect' mental health. Maybe they feel crushingly low from time to time, maybe they wake up every day feeling anxious, maybe they live with the after-effects of trauma, maybe they too have been depressed as fuck (I wish this were the medical term for it) – it really is a mental health spectrum of the broadest kind.

Not only do we have this in common, but we celebrate it (sometimes with dark humour – laughter really can be the best medicine). I love them for their mental health challenges, and they love me for mine. We understand that, to a degree, it makes us who we are, and we embrace ourselves and each other with our 'quirks'. In fact, a friend recently joked with me that she can't relate to people who haven't struggled with their mental health anymore. I thought this an absurd, yet brilliantly funny, exaggeration of the truth, and soon we had an imaginary brand with caps, t-shirts and mugs, emblazoned with, 'All my best friends have mental health issues.' Jokes aside, I feel immensely lucky that I can share in, and embrace, these experiences with my friends.

We often hear about 'normalizing' mental health; the need to remove stigma, so we all feel a little less alone and a little less weird (at least, that's how I like to think of it). By talking openly, the times when our mental health hasn't felt great are normalized – everything from the day we can't get out of bed, to the party we can't bring ourselves to go to because our self-esteem has bolted for the hills, leaving us feeling inadequate. Our struggles are normalized when we hear the real, messy experiences of those around us, helping us curate our own, truer story of what it means to be a human being. By talking about tough feelings, we also model healthy, understanding relationships. We love each other just as much with all our mental health humdingers, and we know that we are no less worthy, likeable or loveable for them. The unexpected, but wonderful, result is that I love myself more because my friends make me feel less weird (though I'm still a proud weirdo, by nature), and the compassion we share among us rubs off and helps me in my own quest for self-compassion.

REASONS TO TALK ABOUT FEELING SHIT

* It makes us feel less alone. We can connect with others who have felt the same. Feeling shit can unite rather than divide us, if we remember to embrace it as a normal part of life. I once made a friend at a work conference because we realized we'd both been depressed! #DepressionFriends

* It helps us feel more supported. When we share, we may expect rejection and derision but often we'll find people asking, 'Is there anything I can do to help?' They might even drag us out for a petrol station ice cream!

* It can help dilute tough feelings. It really is true: a problem shared can be a problem halved. I believe that the power of therapy partly comes from unburdening yourself from the full weight of how you're feeling.

* It can be part of The Plan and catching things early. Telling someone that we feel rubbish isn't necessarily going to stop depression in its tracks. However, talking to a friend about it, and how they then might check in and support us, could help prevent our mood from sinking lower. 'Calling it out' is often the first step towards doing something about it.
* It can make us laugh about it for some light relief! My first therapist always embraced humour as one of our greatest allies in this mind-boggling game of mental health mastery. Some things will simply feel too sad to ever laugh about, but there are those moments, which, viewed from another lens, can be quite comical. Like the time I threw myself on the floor under the sofa to hide from my friends who turned up unannounced, only for them to notice my legs poking out from beneath the furniture when they peered in through the window. Laughing about the more comical moments can make things feel a little lighter.

Speaking as my alter-ego, Ms. Avoid Telling Anyone That I'm Depressed For As Long As I Can Help It, I understand that admitting you're feeling low is easier said than done. I can preach all I like about a spell in depression's dank dungeon being unifying, uplifting and – heaven forbid – funny, if only we'd share. The reality is that the last time I was depressed I couldn't bring myself to tell anyone that I was struggling other than my family (and even that felt hard), let alone gather my besties to say, 'Guess what, gang? I feel shit – and isn't that totally fine!' There are down days, anxious hours and horribly lonely, withdrawn weeks, when depression will be anathema to this so-called connectedness that I've espoused. Finding connection can feel impossible when we're too ashamed to reach out. If this part feels hard, you're not alone.

Mental health is so deeply personal, and it is your experience and your feelings to broadcast, or keep tucked away, as you prefer. But if you can, I'd like you to relieve a bit of pressure from yourself. Feeling shit is normal and you have no cause to feel bad about feeling bad. Finding people to 'share in the shittiness' can be immensely beneficial for your confidence, your self-image and the value you place in yourself. There's no need to wait until you're caught in the thick of it, either. It's always easier when you're feeling better, and you can gather your 'low mood gang' when times are good or bad.

Sharing with the right people, if we feel able to, really can be a lifeline. It soon becomes clear that we've all been through something. What comes back is usually empathy, or a kind curiosity, and a desire to help. If you find sharing your lowest moments too difficult, it's okay to see it as a work in progress. In the meantime, I will gladly take it upon myself to give you this reminder: what you are feeling is not weird or abnormal. Far from it, it makes you about as normal as they come (and isn't that quite a nice feeling?).

The depression hangover

No one likes a hangover, not least the kind depression leaves us with once it's gone in hard and then upped and left. You might be all-too-familiar with the 'depression hangover'. This is the unfortunate result of an emotional energy drain, rather than the type that demands a greasy bacon buttie and a day of TV binge-watching. Not only was depression outstaying its welcome at the party it was never invited to, but it partied hard and drank even harder, with little regard for the repercussions. It arrived with a ton of upheaval in tow and now we're left to manage and cope with the complicated mess left in its wake: the depression hangover.

Over the years, I've realized that depression never feels completely gone, even once our low mood has disappeared. It's not something that gets talked about it. Instead, the perception is that, once we're no longer depressed, we're 'fine'. Though we may be relieved of its immediate symptoms, depression leaves a mark on everything it touches: our sense of self, our identity, our relationships, our confidence, and how we feel about ourselves and our future. I might be 'recovered', but I've never felt as if depression truly left.

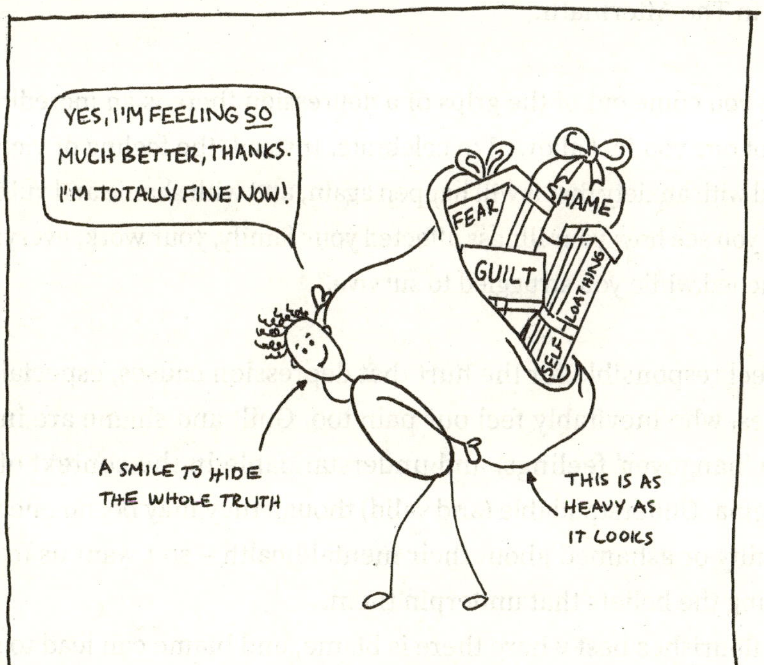

The depression hangover comes with an exhaustive range of particularly uncomfortable negative thoughts and feelings. Guilt, shame, disappointment, self-hatred, disgust, confusion and loneliness are the tip of the iceberg. Mix all that with a good dose of fear that depression may one day return, as we try to get life back on track, and you've got yourself one punchy 'hair of the dog' hangover cocktail.

Someone who's never been depressed might question how or why we could feel so negatively about ourselves once 'recovered'. Not everyone will feel this way, but for many of us who have been depressed, it's a question that feels very easy to answer. I'll go first: I believe I didn't deal with it as well as I could have (in fact, I feel as though I did a totally shit job); I neglected important relationships; I still partly believe depression's narrative that I'm a piece of shit; sometimes I wonder if I *let* this happen and it is my fault after all; I hurt my friends and family; and I don't love the depressed version of myself (though I'm working on that because she absolutely deserves love). You may have similar feelings. It's these thoughts, and innumerable others, that can leave us reeling from depression long after it's gone.

Author, Jenny Lawson, in her book, *Furiously Happy: A Funny Book About Horrible Things*, perfectly encapsulates our complicated relationship with depression in The Aftermath:

> When you come out of the grips of a depression there is an incredible relief, but not one you feel allowed to celebrate. Instead, the feeling of victory is replaced with anxiety that it will happen again, and with shame and vulnerability when you see how your illness affected your family, your work, everything left untouched while you struggled to survive.[9]

We can feel responsible for the hurt that depression causes, especially to our loved ones, who inevitably feel our pain too. Guilt and shame are incredibly common 'hangover' feelings, and understandable in the context of prolific social stigma. Understandable (and valid) though they may be, no one deserves to feel guilty or ashamed about their mental health – so I want us to work on challenging the beliefs that underpin them.

Guilt flourishes best where there is blame, and blame can lead to shame. I have never met someone who has not felt ashamed about their depression at some point. Sadly, we receive so many signs from the world around us – some overt, some subtle – that experiencing mental health issues means there's something shameful and wrong about us. It can feel as if we need to 'get better at good mental health', to prove our worth in the capitalist economies most of us exist within. I'd argue, instead, that we're a convenient scapegoat for governments that don't create systems and environments that work for the many, in all our wonderful diversity – from mental health, to disability, to race, religion and more.

The work required for a societal shift in mental health perspectives is gargantuan and most progress is glacial – we've come on a long way in the last ten years, but there's still an inordinate amount of ground to cover. All the while, my depression hangover rages on. As someone who cannot abide a hangover of any kind, I needed to find a way to feel better about things. How do I feel okay that I am someone who has been depressed? How do I diminish my guilt for the concern, sadness and pain my loved ones felt? How do I accept my identity as 'someone who gets depressed' (still) and does it need to form part of my identity at all? I've had to work hard to find my own voice of truth – over and above what society tells me – to decide, first, what my experiences say about me and, second, how I fit into the world. I've found that it is possible for these two things to co-exist in a way that allows me to let go of much of the negativity I held for so long.

Brené Brown, an academic and podcaster specializing in courage, vulnerability, shame and empathy, has shared a perspective which has guided me when navigating The Aftermath:

> If you put shame in a petri dish and cover it with judgment, silence, and secrecy, you've created the perfect environment for shame to grow... If, on the other hand, you put shame in a petri dish and douse it with empathy, shame loses its power and begins to wither. Empathy creates a hostile environment for shame – an environment it can't survive in, because shame needs you to believe you're alone and it's just you.[10]

Empathy, understanding and acceptance truly are the most potent cure for the depression hangover (but you're welcome to try a Bloody Mary or three raw eggs instead, if that's your thing). Developing this self-directed kindness and love isn't the work of an afternoon, a week or even months. It has taken me years to feel confident in what my depression does and doesn't say about me, and who I truly am – even then, I still have plenty of days when I falter. However, a friend recently reminded me that self-acceptance, in a world which constantly tries to show us our own flaws, is a deeply radical act – we are pushing against the current, and that takes patience, persistence and bravery. I urge you to stick with it, if you can. Nurturing my sense of self has been the singular most valuable thing I've done on this 12-year journey – nothing has brought me more peace.

Along the way, I've arrived at a set of affirmations that I know to be true of myself and anyone who's dealt with depression. They don't prevent the hangover (scientists are still working on that one) but they help me process and dilute those uncomfortable feelings by dousing them in empathy. Think of this as my answer to a restorative bacon sarnie and a day in front of the telly.

Do I still have days when, try as hard as I might, I can't let myself believe any of these things? Absolutely – and no more so than when I've just recovered, as the wounds still feel raw and remnants of my pain linger with stubborn persistence. That pain, in my experience, never goes away completely. We grow alongside it. Some days it feels as if I have a healthy perspective on my past – I understand it and have made my peace with it as best as I can. On others, I feel like a bit of a mess, and I'll cry for all that I've been through and all the time I've lost to depression.

If you are wading through the post-depression quagmire, believing these six affirmations may feel like too much of a stretch – I get that. The important thing is that we remind ourselves that this is our depression hangover beating us up – and it is undeserved. Depression sears it marks into all of us, not least our confidence, and there will undoubtedly be days when we question everything. However, I know that my self-doubt – and yours, too – has it all wrong. I can say that I wholeheartedly believe every single one of those affirmations, and they apply to every person who's been through this – and that includes you. If feeling proud of yourself feels too far off right now, please know that I'm immensely proud of you for pushing through the tough times and still showing up in a world that can feel that bit more daunting, even and especially once we've shown depression the door.

What happens if I ~~relapse~~ get depressed again?

First thing's first, I'm throwing the word 'relapse' in the bin. I respect it as a descriptor that, when used in the context of depression, means that someone has become depressed again. I welcome anyone using it if it feels like a good fit (as always, it's about using language that feels right to us). Personally, I find the word too medicalized, conjuring up an image of a patient who gets sick yet *again*. I'll be using a host of alternative words to explore the prospect of The Depression Comeback Tour (the worst free concert in town).

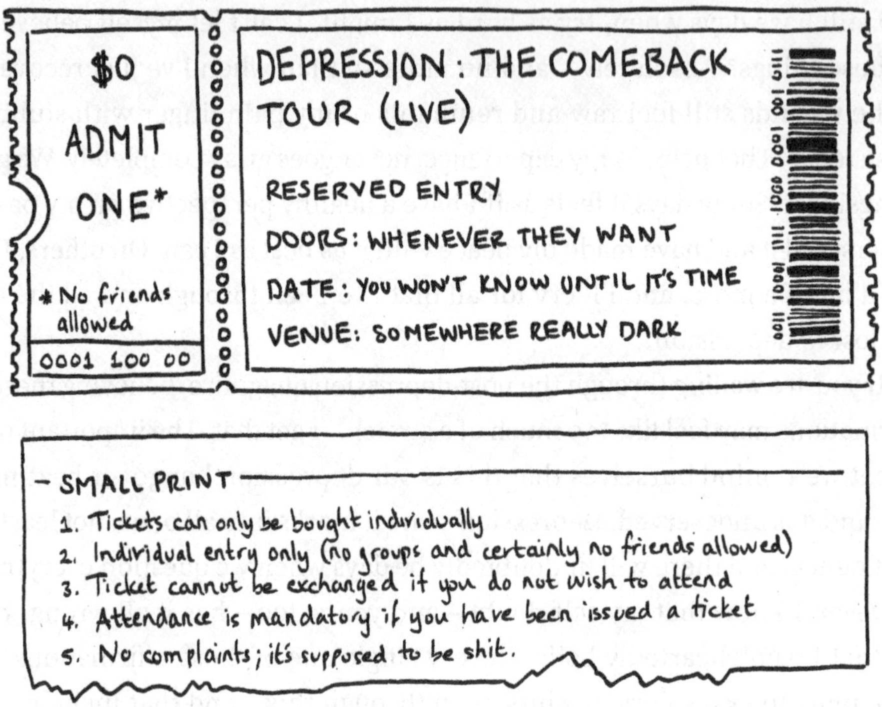

I believe our attitude and approach to our mental health often changes, grows and evolves with time. The same goes for my approach to the possibility of depression returning. At first, I was steadfast in my belief that I'd never see the thing again. Why? First, because I didn't want to think of myself as having a 'condition' or recurring 'problem' (as society would have us perceive it). Second, I didn't know how I'd survive it again, so this felt like an important belief to maintain. Third, I thought if I built an impenetrable mental fortress to its return, it somehow wouldn't be allowed back in. Lastly, I felt that giving into the idea of depression going on the rampage again was to admit defeat and to accept that there was something wrong with me. My belief that depression would never return was a protective one that allowed me to continue with life with a little less fear.

Six dizzying dances with the stuff later, and by the time I came to write this book, I had started to accept that depression could show up again. Should I be smug about the fact that my seventh run-in with depression, before I'd finished writing, proved my point? Who knows, but it did mean that there was no jaw-to-the-floor in total shock this time. It was after this seventh time that I came to a realization: accepting depression, however many times it shows up, was possibly what I needed to forgive myself and relinquish the idea of failure. My denial that depression may well decide to book its comeback tour, for all those years, wasn't protective. Rather, it was giving me reason to blame myself and think I'd 'fucked up' for not keeping it at bay. I must have done something wrong if it was coming back when it 'wasn't supposed to', I believed.

I vowed to change that belief to: life can be really hard and, when it gets on top of me, I may get depressed because it is a *normal response to adverse life conditions* (let me hear you say that last part again!). The only responsibility, or part to play, that I have in depression is to be an active participant in my own recovery. If it decides to practise its boomerang skills, that is not my doing, and I will get through it. I find this approach to depression's rumoured comeback tour to be deeply freeing. Depression is not inevitable, but its possible return becomes normalized and I feel freer of guilt.

That's not to say that I didn't struggle with accepting my most recent tussle with depression; the one that ironically swooped in while I was writing this book on depression (no doubt to prove a point). It crept in imperceptibly – its favourite trick – and had me so under its spell that, even when recovered, I didn't believe I had been depressed because I couldn't drown out the beliefs its lies had left me with. It would take going back to therapy, with some gentle coaxing from my therapist, to finally call it what it really was – depression. Prior to this, there was a phase when I would label it, 'depression, if that's what we're calling it' or I'd gesticulate quotation marks in the air as I said it. Acceptance can be a journey, and we can call our experiences whatever we like while we're making our way forward. Along the way, I still managed to feel shame for that experience, embarrassed that I'd spent months on the sofa and disappeared on my friends yet again.

Of course, I'd choose to never get front row tickets to depression's loathsome show again. In the meantime, I have been able to find a silver lining: I am proud of how I learn and grow each time. I haven't always been able to appreciate those lessons straightaway and often it will all feel totally pointless. However, when depression sets out to create inertia and hopelessness, to identify any growth in the process is the biggest 'Up yours, depression!' we can give. It was only after my seventh depression ding-dong that I decided I felt okay accepting depression as part of my identity – because I'm finally able to do that in a way that feels useful and validating, rather than shameful.

Still, we don't have to learn from depression, nor find any value in it (a simple hatred of the thing is my overriding feeling). In fact, the most important thing I believe you can take from more than one run-in with depression is: *precisely nothing*. I don't want you to read into it, assign any meaning to it, question it or judge yourself for it. Instead, we can aim to explore the reasons why it happened. This helps us build a picture of ourselves and our mood in a way that can help keep us well. Rooting it in a cause adds to our arsenal of evidence that it is not a 'sick' brain that makes us depressed, but a world that can be cruel or circumstances that can be crushing. However, there is no inherent value attached to a repeat run of depression. It simply illustrates what we already know: when life gets hard, our brains might just do what they are programmed to do – a dose of depression. You are no better or worse at depression, or life, if you go through it just the once or a juicy ten times.

As a 'radical' gesture, I propose that, instead, getting depressed (whether it's your first or fifteenth rodeo) demands loving yourself – loving yourself still and maybe even harder than before. I'm sorry you went, or are going through it, again. But you are not your depression; rather, a thinking, feeling human being, with all the wonderful complexity that comes with that.

The brilliant mental health author, Matt Haig, summarizes this perfectly in his book *Reasons to Stay Alive*:

> Depression is smaller than you, even when it feels vast. It operates within you, you do not operate within it. It may be a dark cloud passing across the sky, but – if that is the metaphor – you are the sky. You were there before it. And the cloud can't exist without the sky, but the sky can exist without the cloud.[11]

Depression showing up where it's not wanted again doesn't have to mean anything or 'say' anything about you. It doesn't make you bad or weak, a failure or a disappointment. We get to decide how we identify, and whether we make depression a part of that or not. We get to choose how we want to envisage our future and what we think of our own mental health.

You are that magical sky – on the days that there are dark clouds and on the days that there aren't. You are not your depression.

* **CHAPTER 15** *

You Deserve to Feel Proud

As we near the end of our time together, you'll probably have a sense of the journey I've been on, and just how much that journey means to me. For all the light-heartedness and 'fun' I aim to inject into the topic (let's face it, depression is depressing enough in itself), there is nothing else in my life that feels more profound, more emotional, more saddening and – I'll say it – more *unfair* than depression.

For something I loathe, it holds an unrivalled importance in my life. I don't like depression, but I also treasure the things it has given me. The way I've learnt to deal with it, the lessons it has taught me about life, the care and compassion I have had to learn to treat myself with, the way that I'm able to extend that to others, and the incredible people (and their stories) that it has brought into my life.

So, you might understand how difficult this ending feels. How do I sum up something that feels completely beyond words?

Perhaps you remember that red thread of connection that I talked about at the start. It runs between me and every other person I've met who has had depression. I see them and I understand, and sometimes even feel, their pain. I know we haven't met, but that red thread now stretches out in a somewhat tangled mess to all of you. I've never given as much advice about depression, never told so much of my story, never thought so deeply so I can explain my experience in a way that helps others, as I have done for this book. You and I may never have met, but, as I write these words, I feel as if we have, my red thread crew.

As that link runs between me and you, I ask myself, what would I want to tell myself at the end of all of this? Wherever you are on your journey – still confused after your first go at depression or a weary depression dance master – what will you find helpful? I hope the points I'm about to share will only be reinforcing the concepts you've become familiar with as we've travelled along together.

There is nothing wrong with you

From the bottom of my heart, I want you to know – and believe (sometimes that's the hardest part) – that there is nothing wrong with you. Short of getting out a science textbook, I can only impress on you one final time that we are designed to get depressed when things get too much for us; it is how our brains are wired and an *understandable response to adverse life conditions*. Of course, it is still entirely shitty that we've been through it, when others may never even get a sniff of the stuff. Perhaps we are 'better' at getting depression than others, or maybe life has dealt us some harder knocks – we"ll never know for sure. But whether you've been through it once, or ten times, it is normal. Now, all together, repeat after me: 'My depression makes me normal!'

You are not alone

If it is normal, that means that we are not alone in any of this.

As soon as I started being open about my depression – talking to friends, posting on social media and eventually giving talks about it – I realized just how many people have had a dance or two or ten with that least desirable of dance partners. I'm pleased to report that it doesn't make us special. Depression will tell us that we are the only horrific person in the world like this, but – what do we know about depression? It lies, and the idea that we are alone in this is just another one of its tiresome, dull lies.

Of course, society does a great job at nurturing shame, which perpetuates

a repressive silence around our mental health. How can we know that we share this experience with others if we feel that we have a huge secret we must keep, for fear that we'll be judged if word gets out? If you're feeling this way, you could try mentioning it to a couple of trusted friends, finding relevant social media accounts or having a look on online forums. There are tons of us. We're the least unique and special people alive, if you want to look at it that way (and isn't that wonderful?).

It can feel difficult to find and connect with others. If you'd like to join a community of people who 'get it', following me on social media (more details are on my website, which you can find at the back of the book) will present you with a ready-made group of people who all care about, and understand, depression. I'd love for you to come and join us.

There is no right or wrong

I've grown with every depression encounter. My seventh, and most recent, liaison with the stuff taught me yet another lesson: you can't 'do depression' correctly or incorrectly. There really is no right or wrong, no singular standard we should be aiming for, nor rules that we should be abiding by.

Internalizing this belief has helped me more than almost anything else. I used to assess myself very negatively when out the other side of another period of low mood. I felt that if I were 'better at depression', I'd have lifted myself out of it quicker or stopped it taking hold in the first place. In reality, we could be acting on hundreds of hare-brained schemes to give depression a clip round the ear, or just having a go at one; it doesn't make any approach 'right' or 'wrong'. What works for one person may not work for you or what worked for you last time may fall flat this time (and that's okay too!).

A good rule of thumb is that there simply are no absolutes. If someone has hauled themselves out of a depression hole in a way that would never work for you, all power to them! How great that they've found their thing. Equally, if what you're trying isn't working, and you're feeling hopeless, that doesn't mean you're doing it wrong or failing – the skill in all of this is trying and learning, and then trying again.

There is no black and white in this game, only shades of grey that we muddle through. You're not doing anything wrong – that simply isn't possible.

You're doing your best, and that is amazing

Not only are you not doing anything wrong, but, if you are trying, that is enough. You're doing your best and that truly is amazing. Some days, that might look like dragging yourself out of the house to read a book in a cafe, rather than your body slowly fusing at a molecular level with the sofa. Other days, it might be recognizing and honouring the need to have more of a 'nothingy' day because that's what feels manageable. Both, and everything in-between, are more than good enough. You are brilliant for withstanding it.

All I ask is that you don't give up. You'll have felt as if you've thrown in the towel, or have been on the cusp of it, countless times – but you haven't really. Depression isn't your fault, there's nothing 'wrong' with experiencing it, but you deserve to live a life in which you feel freer from it, if you can.

I appreciate that it's not always that simple. For some, depression will be the first thing they're greeted by when they open their eyes every morning. I understand how relentless and inescapable that feels. My belief is that, even in those circumstances, we deserve to make incremental gains to feel a little better and live the best life we can (which might be better than we realize, if we've felt low for a very long time). Maybe just going for a daily walk, or chatting to a friend once a week, makes us feel a bit better. Or, maybe, it starts us on a recovery journey we didn't know we're capable of.

Owning our right to feeling better can be complicated, but you deserve so much from your life. It is a journey, and it takes time and practice. But if you are trying, or have intentions, to get to a place where you feel lighter – I'll say it again – that is enough, and it is amazing.

* * *

These are the truths that I want you to be left with when you turn the last page of this book. On the face of it, this book is about how to tell depression to leave you alone (maybe with a few more expletives) and bid it a not-so-polite farewell. However, you might have noticed that I'm not closing this book by reminding you of all the tips and tricks you could use to never see depression again. That's because, while I have tried to offer some helpful advice, I don't have all the answers. I can't present you with a sure-fire way to get rid of depression – no one can.

What I do know is that depression can steal huge amounts of our confidence, sometimes every ounce of it. We can be left feeling like a compromised human, doubting our abilities, our future and our reliability, in work, relationships and more. We might wonder how long we've got before depression decides to show its ugly face again. We'll probably feel like a bad friend if we've withdrawn, or like a burden for needing support. Everything is called into question once you've had depression, and our confidence bears the brunt of that effect.

Thankfully, confidence can be found again.

I am here to tell you that you are doing just fine. Scrap that, you're doing brilliantly. My one wish would be that every single one of you can live your life, feeling that bit more prepared to take on depression, but – more than anything

– that you know your own magic, and that it has nothing to do with the state of your mental health. I wish for your confidence to shimmy through that sticky patch of low mood, and the rest of life, with all the pizzazz and glamour of Ru Paul's finest drag queens, strutting through life as if it's your catwalk.

As for me, I will do anything I can to piss off depression. What I have come to learn over these many years is that there is nothing depression hates more than confidence and loving ourselves – radically and relentlessly. So, let depression do its worst. We can get through it, together, guided by a communal love, empathy and understanding – for ourselves and each other. And, not only that, I can see all our wonder; we are fantastic, with or without depression. That is your truth, and I am proud of you.

Acknowledgements

This is a thank you of two kinds. It is a thank you to the wonderful people in my life who supported me every step of the way in this dream of mine to 'turn shit into gold' (thank you to my writing teacher, Kerry, for summing it up so perfectly). Without them, I certainly wouldn't have this book – which means more to me than words can describe.

It is also profoundly more than that – this is a thank you to my very own support crew. They are an incredible bunch of human beings who have supported me on my mental health journey. They are the ones who have made any of this remotely manageable. I'd have been lost without them.

So, this is a heartfelt thank you to the people whose love and support breathed this very story to life alongside me.

* * *

To my therapists. There is no Jacs the Badass Mental Health Master without the therapy I had with my first therapist, Julia. It gave me the foundations to grow around depression and helped me realize that I will always be bigger and better than it. Having the unwavering support of such a big ally along the way has meant everything. The version of me that continues to evolve and reflect on her journey with ever-increasing clarity, maturity and self-compassion (when I can manage it!) has grown from 'doing the work' with the support of my most recent therapist, Natalie. Thank you to both of you for being part of my growth.

To my friends. To every friend along the way who has ever texted me, called me or thought about me when depression has had me deep in a hole and very much 'missing in action', I am so immensely grateful for you all. I've only been able to mention a few in the book (Tash, Karlia and Kezia are all real people!) but I feel that I have an army of the most incredible human beings behind me. I hated you for turning up at my door unannounced when I was depressed, but I bloody love you for it now. Thank you for always being there and for learning on this journey with me.

To my partner, Carmel. You are in all the days I pushed through the ups and downs, the beauty and the challenges, that writing this book has brought. And if we ever have to tackle depression together – I know we'll be just fine. Thank you for always being my biggest supporter.

To my family – Mum, Dad and Nic. There are some things words simply cannot do justice to. My biggest thank you goes to you. I love you all.

The hardest of journeys are best walked with the very best of people. Thank you to everyone who has been part of mine. I'm so glad I never gave up.

* * *

I'd like to thank my publisher, Jessica Kingsley Publishers, and my editor, Jane, for believing that my drawings, words and a bunch of mental health holes have the power to transform how we think about our mental health. Because they really do.

Recommended Resources

To accompany the advice and guidance in the book, I've suggested that there are a plethora of support groups and resources that we can look to, to help us find new support avenues – or just group activities to do with our depressed selves (where we might even find our support crew)! While Google is always your best friend, I wanted to provide a few to get you started.

Below, I've shared a few key resources to turn to – either because they provide excellent all-round support, or because they can help if support is required more urgently. As I am a Brit, these have a UK focus, but many have written articles and resources that will help anyone.

The rest of my recommended resources, groups and organizations can be found on my website: **www.jacsguderley.com/resources**.

There, you'll find a greater variety of options, as well as some country-specific recommendations, for my international red thread crew!

Lastly, if you're looking for more details of a specific type of group or support that I mentioned within the book, look to the end of this list.

Urgent support

First and foremost, if you feel that you might attempt suicide, or may have seriously harmed yourself, please seek urgent medical help.

* In the UK, call 999 for an ambulance.
* Go straight to A&E, if you can.
* Call your local crisis team, if you have their number.

If you can keep yourself safe for a while, and don't want to call 999, contact NHS 111 England or NHS 111 Wales (select option 2 to access a 24/7 helpline that offers urgent mental health support). Or you can call your GP and ask for an emergency appointment.

If you need to talk right now (whether you're at risk of harming yourself or not), there are always people available:

* Call Samaritans on 116 123 www.samaritans.org/how-we-can-help/contact-samaritan (UK-wide)
* Text SHOUT to 85258 https://giveusashout.org (UK-wide)
* Call CALL on 0800 132 737 www.callhelpline.org.uk (Wales only)

Suicide support

* **Campaign Against Living Miserably (CALM): www.thecalmzone.net**

  Provides a helpline, online and WhatsApp chat, as well as information and support, for anyone affected by suicide or suicidal thoughts.

* **Staying Safe: www.stayingsafe.net**

  Provides vital guidance tools – with easy to print/online templates and video tutorials – to help people write their own suicide 'Safety Plan', to build hope and identify actions and strategies to resist suicidal thoughts.

* **Andy's Man Club: https://andysmanclub.co.uk**

  A men's suicide prevention charity, offering free-to-attend, peer-to-peer support groups across the UK and online.

General mental health support (UK)

* **Mind (mental health charity): www.mind.org.uk**
* **SANE: www.sane.org.uk**
* **SupportLine: www.supportline.org.uk**

* **Depression UK: www.depressionuk.org**

Mental health support groups

* **Rethink Mental Illness: www.rethink.org/help-in-your-area/about-services-and-groups**

  Over 130+ local support groups which are run by people with experience of mental illness. These are welcoming, non-judgemental spaces in which you can talk openly about your experiences and receive support.

* **Mind's peer support guide: www.mind.org.uk/information-support/guides-to-support-and-services/peer-support-groups**

  Information and advice on finding a peer support group for you, including links to Mind's own initiatives.

* **Mind's Side by Side: https://sidebyside.mind.org.uk**

  An online peer support community where you can talk about your mental health and connect with others who understand what you're going through.

* **Mental health UK: https://mentalhealth-uk.org/partnerships/projects/support-groups**

  Mental health support groups aimed at combatting loneliness. Members come together to discuss their experiences in a safe space, take part in activities and share information. Activities range from sport and leisure to gardening, cooking, dog walking and attending relevant talks.

* **The Hub of Hope: https://hubofhope.co.uk**

  Hub of Hope is the UK's largest mental health support directory. It brings local, national, peer, community, charity, private and NHS mental health support services together in one place.

LGBTQIA+ support (UK)

* **Consortium: www.consortium.lgbt/member-directory**

  The largest network of LGBQTIA+ groups and organizations in the UK. This directory of their members lists groups that range from charities to book clubs, pride organizations, youth groups and more.

* **Stonewall: www.stonewall.org.uk/resources/support-services-in-the-sector**

  A UK-based charity that works to advance the rights and equality of LGBTQIA+ people. It lists a wide range of organizations, services and helplines that offer support.

* **Switchboard: https://switchboard.lgbt**

  A support line (phone, email and online chat) to discuss anything related to sexuality and gender identity.

* **Gender Identity Research & Education Society (GIRES): www.gires.org.uk**

  A UK-wide organization to improve the lives of trans and gender diverse people of all ages, including those who are non-binary and non-gender.

Other references in the text

Find events and meet others

If you'd like to meet others with shared experiences, try typing 'mental health' or 'depression' into the search bar. Or you could simply search for a hobby or interest that takes your fancy!

* Meetup: www.meetup.com
* Eventbrite: www.eventbrite.co.uk
* Queer events
  * » OutSavvy: www.outsavvy.com
  * » Consortium: www.consortium.lgbt/events

Understanding therapy options

* **The British Association for Counselling and Psychotherapy (BACP): www.bacp.co.uk/about-therapy/types-of-therapy**

  An extensive A–Z of therapeutic approaches, explaining the different beliefs and approaches behind each one.

Accessing therapy

* **Advice from Mind on 'How to find therapy or counselling': www.mind.org.uk/information-support/drugs-and-treatments/talking-therapy-and-counselling/how-to-find-a-therapist**

Therapist directories

When using online therapy directories, I'd recommend choosing based on a combination of factors: do they offer the type of therapy you're interested in? Do they list the issue you're struggling with most (e.g. depression) in their areas of expertise? Do they offer online and/or in-person sessions? Do you get a good feel about them from the description they've written?

* British Association for Counselling and Psychotherapy (UK only): www.bacp.co.uk/about-therapy/using-our-therapist-directory
* UK Council for Psychotherapy (UK only): www.psychotherapy.org.uk
* Psychology Today (worldwide): www.psychologytoday.com/gb/counselling (select your desired country)

Volunteering opportunities

Getting in touch with a local charity (pick up the phone or just pop into a shop on your high street next time you're passing by!) is a great way to explore volunteering opportunities. For more options, there are some great resources online:

* **Timebanking UK: https://timebanking.org/find-your-nearest-time-bank**

  Help someone for an hour (or thereabouts) – for example by mowing their lawn or doing their shopping. For every hour of help you give, you earn an hour's credit from your time bank, and you can spend your time credit by receiving an hour of someone else's time.

* **NCVO: www.ncvo.org.uk (England only)**

  A membership community for charities, voluntary organizations and community groups in England, championing voluntary action.

* **Volunteering Matters: https://volunteeringmatters.org.uk**

  A charity on a mission to create a brighter future for communities across the UK through the power of volunteering.

Socially and culturally sensitive support

On my website's resource page (www.jacsguderley.com/resources), I recommend a number of social and cultural-specific groups and resources. For example, but not limited to:

* **The Silver Line: www.thesilverline.org.uk**

  A support line for those aged 55 and above.

* **South Asian Therapists: https://southasiantherapists.org**

  A directory of South Asian therapists.

* **Men Who Talk: https://menwhotalk.org**

  Supporting men to achieve good mental health through the medium of chat.

* **Black Minds Matter UK: https://www.blackmindsmatteruk.com/**

  A registered charity connecting Black individuals and families with free 121 talking therapy delivered by qualified and accredited Black therapists. They also provide useful resources.

* **The Black, African and Asian Therapy Network: https://www.baatn.org.uk/**

  The largest community of Counsellors and Psychotherapists of Black, African, Asian and Caribbean Heritage in the UK.

* **WISH: https://www.womenatwish.org.uk/**

  A user-led women's mental health charity developing pioneering support services for under-served women and campaigning together for social justice.

* **Sense: https://www.sense.org.uk/**

  A UK charity that supports disabled people with complex needs to feel connected and included.

Join me online!

I like to share my thoughts on depression and mental health online, too. On my socials, you'll find a bunch of people who get what it's like to struggle with their mental health, or who have supported someone with their mental health. Come and join us – I'd love to see you there!

* Instagram: @mysketchyhead (www.instagram.com/mysketchyhead)
* TikTok: @mysketchyhead (www.tiktok.com/@mysketchyhead)
* My website: www.jacsguderley.com

Endnotes

1 Roosevelt, F.D. (1938) 'A smooth sea never made a skilled sailor.' Fireside Chat radio broadcast, 14 April 1938.

2 Moncrieff, J., Cooper, R.E., Stockmann, T. *et al.* (2022) 'The serotonin theory of depression: A systematic umbrella review of the evidence.' *Molecular Psychiatry*, 28, 3243–3256. Accessed on 05/04/2025 at https://doi.org/10.1038/s41380-022-01661-0

3 World Health Organization (n.d.) Depression. World Health Organization. Accessed on 18/05/2025 at www.who.int/health-topics/depression

4 Moncrieff, J. & Kirsch, I. (2015) 'Empirically derived criteria cast doubt on the clinical significance of antidepressant-placebo differences.' *Contemporary Clinical Trials*, 43, 60–62. Accessed on 05/04/2025 at https://doi.org/10.1016/j.cct.2015.05.005

5 Cipriani, A. *et al.* (2018) 'Comparative efficacy and acceptability of 21 antidepressant drugs for the acute treatment of adults with major depressive disorder: A systematic review and network meta-analysis.' *The Lancet*, 391, 10128, 1357–1366. Accessed on 22/03/2025 at https://doi.org/10.1016/S0140-6736(17)32802-7

6 Gen, Li *et al.* (2023) 'Understanding the protective effect of social support on depression symptomatology from a longitudinal network perspective.' *BMJ Mental Health*, 26(1), 1–7. Accessed on 22/03/2025 at https://doi.org/10.1136/bmjment-2023-300802

7 Lambert, M.J. & Barley, D.E. (2001) 'Research summary on the therapeutic relationship and psychotherapy outcome.' *Psychotherapy: Theory, Research,*

Practice, Training, 38(4), 357–361. Accessed on 22/03/2025 at https://doi.org/10.1037/0033-3204.38.4.357

8 Murakami, H. (2005) *Kafka on the Shore*. London: Vintage Publishing, p.5.

9 Lawson, J. (2015) *Furiously Happy: A Funny Book About Horrible Things*. New York: Flatiron Books, p.317.

10 Brown, B. (2018) *Dare to Lead: Brave Work. Tough Conversations. Whole Hearts*. New York: Random House, p.41.

11 Haig, M. (2015) *Reasons to Stay Alive*. New York: Penguin Books, p.181.

RAISING READERS
Books Build Bright Futures

Dear Reader,

We'd love your attention for one more page to tell you about the crisis in children's reading, and what we can all do.

Studies have shown that reading for fun is the **single biggest predictor of a child's future life chances** – more than family circumstance, parents' educational background or income. It improves academic results, mental health, wealth, communication skills, ambition and happiness.[1]

The number of children reading for fun is in rapid decline. Young people have a lot of competition for their time. In 2024, 1 in 10 children and young people in the UK aged 5 to 18 did not own a single book at home.[2]

Hachette works extensively with schools, libraries and literacy charities, but here are some ways we can all raise more readers:

- Reading to children for just 10 minutes a day makes a difference
- Don't give up if children aren't regular readers – there will be books for them!
- Visit bookshops and libraries to get recommendations
- Encourage them to listen to audiobooks
- Support school libraries
- Give books as gifts

There's a lot more information about how to encourage children to read on our website: **www.RaisingReaders.co.uk**

Thank you for reading.

hachette UK

1 OECD, '21st-Century Readers: Developing Literacy Skills in a Digital World', 2021, https://www.oecd.org/en/publications/21st-century-readers_a83d84cb-en.html

2 National Literacy Trust, 'Book Ownership in 2024', November 2024, https://literacytrust.org.uk/research-services/research-reports/book-ownership-in-2024